D0894358

DISCARDED

WIDENER UNIVERSITY

TEACHING INTERNATIONAL POLITICS IN HIGH SCHOOL

Teaching International Politics
in High School

Edited by
Raymond English

ETHICS AND PUBLIC POLICY CENTER

THE **ETHICS AND PUBLIC POLICY CENTER,** established in 1976, conducts a program of research, writing, publications, and conferences to encourage debate on domestic and foreign policy issues among religious, educational, academic, business, political, and other leaders. A nonpartisan effort, the Center is supported by contributions (which are tax deductible) from foundations, corporations, and individuals. The authors alone are responsible for the views expressed in Center publications. The founding president of the Center is **Ernest W. Lefever.**

Library of Congress Cataloging-in-Publication Data

Teaching international politics in high school.
1. International relations—Study and teaching (Secondary)—United States.
I. English, Raymond.
JX1293.U6T426   1989
327'.071'273   89–1250
ISBN 0–89633–137–7 (alk. paper)
ISBN 0–89633–138–5 (pbk.: alk. paper)

Distributed by arrangement with:

University Press of America, Inc.
4720 Boston Way
Lanham, MD 20706

3 Henrietta Street
London WC2E 8LU England

All Ethics and Public Policy Center books are produced on acid-free paper. The paper used in this publication meets the minimum requirements of American National Standard for Information Sciences—Permanence of Paper for Printed Library Materials, ANSI Z39.48–1984.   ∞

© 1989 by the Ethics and Public Policy Center. All rights reserved.
Printed in the United States of America.

Ethics and Public Policy Center
1030 Fifteenth Street N.W.
Washington, D.C. 20005
(202) 682–1200

WIDENER UNIVERSITY
WOLFGRAM
LIBRARY
CHESTER, PA.

Contents

Foreword

RAYMOND ENGLISH

INTERNATIONAL POLITICS—the power relations among states—is generally neglected in pre-college education. Many of our young people receive high school diplomas despite an appalling ignorance of the basic facts of geography, foreign affairs, and U.S. defense policies. Such ignorance endangers the future of our self-governing republic.

Democratic societies are traditionally at a disadvantage compared with oligarchic or dictatorial regimes. The reasons are many and obvious, but in recent decades they have been compounded by enormous technological changes. In the past, for example, after a sudden onslaught, democracies enjoyed a breathing space during which their people could arm and defend themselves against the foreign menace. Such was the case of Britain in both World War I and World War II, and of the United States after Pearl Harbor.

Today, this breathing space is dramatically diminished. Already in 1939, the Germans were able to overrun Poland in a single month, and in 1940, Norway and France were defeated by German troops in a matter of weeks. Today, moreover, aggressive powers challenge democracies not so much by direct as by indirect attack—subversion, propaganda, terrorism—all of which undermine the power and prestige of their victims.

Thus the democratic United States was faced with the imminent Communist subversion of Greece in 1948, with the Berlin Blockade in 1949, and with the North Korean invasion of South Korea in 1950. In the early 1960s, nearby Cuba became a Soviet outpost; in 1978, Nicaragua was doomed to the same fate (Grenada was rescued from Soviet-Cuban control in 1984 only by U.S. intervention). In Africa and the Middle East, the influence of Western powers has been threatened by direct military might, but also by subversion and terrorism in some countries, and by the installation of pro-Soviet regimes in others: Ethiopia, Angola, Mozambique, Iraq, and Syria. Communism has also spread to Vietnam, Laos, Cambodia, and Afghanistan; and it may yet find a foothold in Iran.

These international crises demonstrate the difficulties democracies face in maintaining an informed public, both willing and able to counter the ambitions of expansionist powers. Post-World War II history highlights the need for young Americans to understand the constant threat to the free world.

In meeting this need, the teachers in our public high schools face a double task: (1) to enable students to understand what is required to prevent a confrontation between the superpowers or their allies (the North Atlantic Treaty Organization and Warsaw Pact); and (2) to enable students to appreciate the complexities of the global balance of power.

Some educators have responded well to these challenges. They realize that free societies are endangered and that they can remain free and prevent major wars only by intelligent defensive measures. These teachers offer students a realistic view of international affairs. Even when they disagree with U.S. foreign policy, they do not exclude it from their curricula.

By contrast, many elementary and secondary schools have bowed in recent years to pressure groups and have adopted instructional materials clearly designed to further "peace" at any cost.

For example, many courses on "nuclear weapons" or "nuclear war" have appeared. Yet the materials used in these courses have little to do with the foreign and defense policies of the United States and its allies, and even less with the policies of the Soviet Union and its satellites. Many of the materials even neglect essential facts—that only two atomic weapons have ever been used, and that there have been some two hundred conventional wars since then. Rarely is it pointed out that the free world's nuclear arsenal may actually have *prevented* major war for over forty years.

These materials, many of which are privately produced, view public "education" as a process of indoctrinating students, rather than teaching them objective facts and developing their skills. For these "educators," concern with the grim details of international politics, with *realpolitik,* seems a betrayal of their vocation.

Another obstacle to teaching controversial topics is semantic: the tendency to use code words understood only by the initiated. Thus the apparently precise term *values* actually means *opinions, inclinations, personal preferences,* and is meant to substitute for the unpalatable terms *good/bad, right/wrong.* As a result, great moral principles are trivialized in the classroom. Similarly, *critical thinking* often means the rejection of traditional standards of judging right and wrong, and *conflict resolution* means treating all nations, all national policies, all ideas, and all ethical principles as morally neutral or equal. There are many similar examples.

This technique of using codewords is as old as the Sophists whom Plato and Socrates criticized. More recently, it was brought to a fine art by the Stalinists, and it remains an effective instrument for confusing issues despite Orwell's brilliant satires in *Animal Farm* ("All animals are equal, but some are more equal than others") and *1984* ("War is Peace; Slavery is Freedom.") To be sure, many teachers are unaware of the moral pitfalls resulting from these ideologically charged terms.

Politics is by definition concerned with power. The very term *international politics* emphasizes organized power and conflicts in the world. International politics should not be primarily concerned with culture, as worthy as this is, but with the relationships between complex organized human groups that generate power, ideas, and interests. The question of power remains central to the study of a presidential election in the United States, the Soviet invasion of Afghanistan, or Hitler's near conquest of both Europe and the Soviet Union.

"Strength" involves more than military might. Though military power is essential for any government, economic and moral strength is also indispensable. As one of our authors indicates, the "trading state" is a major component of contemporary international relations. Economically healthy states are able to gain allies and influence many nations through the voluntary exchange of goods, business personnel, and investment, as well as by direct gifts and loans. Economic strength also undergirds military power.

The moral component is vital in free nations because effective foreign policy depends on the intelligence and will of the people in a democracy. Even in totalitarian dictatorships, morale is ultimately crucial; there is a point at which coercion, surveillance, censorship, and propaganda cease to be effective. There can be little doubt, for example, that uncertainty about the loyalty of certain ethnic groups within the Soviet Union and its satellite countries restrains Soviet expansionist aims.

Democracies are at a disadvantage in the competition of international politics. Their handicap stems first from popular ignorance of the issues, and the ignorance is often compounded by sentimentality. Whether education can remedy this is debatable. This volume asks three questions. Can anything be done? what should be done? and how should it be done? It also seeks to provide some answers to these questions, which are of vital importance to the survival of America's experiment in the self-governance of a free people.

A final caution. In any political situation, there is doubtless a best (or least bad) and a worst policy. Human wisdom, however, is seldom capable of selecting unerringly the best. Democracies generally face a number of options, and only the necessity for taking decisive action will resolve the debate in a given case. Consequently readers will find a variety of points of view in the following pages, and will no doubt apply the ideas most suited to the schools and classrooms they know.

Post Script to Foreword

Readers may feel that the changes in the Soviet Union in the late 1980s are neglected in the following pages. Indeed, most of the material here was assembled before the INF Treaty, the revelations of economic breakdown in the USSR, and the experiments in *glasnost* and *perestroika*. But the significance of these developments remains uncertain.

America, the World, and Our Schools

WILLIAM J. BENNETT

FOR SEVERAL YEARS I have urged renewed attention to American history in our nation's schools. Too many of our students now pass through school without gaining a firm grounding in the principles of our liberal democracy. If they are to become good citizens—and preparing them for democratic citizenship is among our schools' most important responsibilities—then our children must know the lessons of American history. They must also know about world history, and about the issues confronting the world today.

Does the larger world have a place in American education and especially in education for democratic citizenship? In fact, it does and always has. As Abraham Lincoln remarked, every American's schooling should equip him "to read the histories of his own *and other* countries, by which he may duly appreciate the value of our free institutions."

During Lincoln's time American students read these histories, and doing so taught them the most important lesson of international politics. That lesson is that their own system of government is different from and nominally superior to most of the systems of government elsewhere in the world. They learned, too, that from the inception of our republic, Americans have hoped that their experiment in self-rule would ultimately benefit

William J. Bennett was secretary of education during the second Reagan administration. He was chairman of the National Endowment for the Humanities in the first administration. He earned degrees from Williams College, the University of Texas, and Harvard Law School, and has received numerous honorary degrees. Before joining the Reagan administration, he directed the National Humanities Center in North Carolina.

1

people everywhere in the world. "The institutions of the United States," wrote Lord Bryce in 1888, "are believed to disclose and display the type of institutions towards which, as by a law of fate, the rest of civilized mankind are forced to move, some with swifter, others with slower, but all with unresting feet."

The Role of Our Schools

Some of this hope has been rewarded, but not everyone has followed our lead. Europe, for example, is divided today between examples left by the unresting feet of democracy and examples stamped by the rougher boots of occupying armies and regimes hostile to free institutions. It is within a world of such contrasts and conflicts that the United States finds itself a global power. Our global responsibilities and the realities of international politics have a more pressing claim on our attention than ever before. We therefore need to know—and pass on to our children—as much about the world as we possibly can. The question is, how well are public schools performing this task?

On first inspection, perhaps not altogether badly. Of course, new technologies have helped. When a movement for democracy took hold in the Philippines in February 1987, for example, Americans (and American children) saw its leaders interviewed on television—even before their victory had been secured. Through the technology of television, our children see summit meetings, Ayatollahs, hostages, and Soviet tanks rumbling through Afghanistan.

There is other evidence of a more formal effort. For secondary schools, new social studies curricula are being developed by men and women who are mindful that the American electorate must be knowledgeable about foreign policy. In higher education, international politics has become a distinctive discipline. In 1976, for example, American universities awarded as many Ph.D.'s in international studies as they had in the first forty years of this century.

But this evidence is deceptive and may not indicate true knowledge of the subject. Furthermore, relatively few Americans hold a Ph.D. in international studies. There is no guarantee that even those who do will see the world as it truly is. So the crucial questions remain: how much do *most* American students know about the world we live in? how well do Americans understand the fundamental character of international politics today—that our republican form of government stands for certain things in the world, and that other regimes stand against us?

Freedom and Totalitarianism

Do our students understand that the United States represents something more than the interests of a big power in global competition? That our international posture reflects our founding principles. That we stand as a free, self-governing society in defense of those ideas that together make for freedom and self-government—ideas such as respect for the individual, religious freedom, the rule of law, limited government, private property, the freely given, uncoerced consent of the governed? Do our students understand American rights to dissent such as the freedoms of speech, press, association, and assembly? What of majority rule? And do they understand that these ideas are not shared throughout the world, and that, in some places, though they are honored in theory, they are dishonored in practice?

How well do our students understand that, in the present international arrangement, there exists another general idea of government, one backed by considerable armed strength? It is an aggressive idea that does not shrink from the use of that strength, and it is an idea of near total darkness. In the areas to which it has spread, not a single ideal that Americans believe to be universal, good, and beyond dispute still shines—except, of course, in the hearts of its bravest victims.

The twenty-fifth anniversary of the erection of the Berlin Wall occurred in 1986. Year after year, men and women are still willing to risk death to cross over this wall from East to West to breathe the air of freedom. They do not often succeed. Not long ago, a young man attempting to escape to the West reached the top of the wall, only to be cut down in a hail of machine-gun bullets. Witnesses then heard an East German border guard yell, "I got you, you swine," at the young man's corpse. Another

East German guard, unable to countenance the murder, shouted back at his colleagues in disgust. The protesting guard was quickly disarmed and led away, God only knows where.

Are we teaching young Americans to understand the Berlin Wall's history and significance? When East Germany's dictator Erich Honecker calls the wall an "anti-fascist protective rampart," do students know this is doublespeak? Do they know what "dictatorship of the proletariat" means? Can they grasp that a totalitarian state recognizes no inviolable individual rights? Are they familiar with planned liquidations? Do they realize that some governments use terror as an instrument of state policy? Do they know of the NKVD and KGB, of induced famines, purges, show trials, pacts with Hitler, and the Gulag? Do our students know the fate of Cambodia? Are they aware of current developments in Ethiopia? Can they therefore see why free men and women resist the expansion of Communism around the world?

Evidence of Ignorance

There is reason to doubt that we are successfully educating Americans about these large facts of the modern world. The Southern Governors Association in late 1986, for example, issued a report that documented the "international illiteracy" in America's schools and revealed that 20 per cent of sixth-grade students surveyed could not locate the United States on a map. There is evidence of similar ignorance among secondary school students in a 1985 survey by the National Assessment of Educational Progress, which revealed that American eleventh-graders knew astonishingly little of their own history. Two-thirds of them could not place the Civil War in the correct half-century; one-third of them failed the same test for the Declaration of Independence, for Columbus, and for World War I; nearly a third could not say which two nations were our principal enemies in World War II; and half of them were unfamiliar with the names Winston Churchill and Joseph Stalin.

These last examples should concern us most; if half our students, in a casual conversation, could conceivably hear Stalin's crimes attributed to Winston Churchill and not know the difference, then they do not understand what they need to about contemporary international politics. They are, in Professor Paul Gagnon's words, "unarmed for public discourse."

This is not to criticize our children. If they do not know these things, it is in most cases not their fault. The blame falls on those of us whose job it is to educate American children. Responsibility for redressing the failure is ours as well. How can we do so? By emphasizing facts, for one thing. In our secondary schools there is no shortage of curricula for the teaching of international politics, but in general they do not pay sufficient attention to facts. Sometimes even their basic premises are non-factual.

"Peace" Propaganda In Our Schools

Consider the various "nuclear age" or "peace" curricula. These begin with the assumption that American children are terrified by the prospect of nuclear annihilation. As it happens, there is no reliable polling evidence for this claim—in fact, students are much more worried about drugs than nuclear war—but to the advocates of such curricula this just proves the depth of children's terror, which, they say, has been completely repressed.

As "therapy," the nuclear age and peace curricula attempt to bring the fear out in the open. Students are made to watch graphic films of victims from the Hiroshima and Nagasaki bombings. They play games in which they contemplate their own deaths. They draw concentric circles on maps of their own neighborhoods to simulate the geography of destruction from nuclear explosion. But does fear foster prevention? Does panic foster knowledge? Will the vision of apocalyptic war usher in an age of utopian peace? Is this the sort of education in international politics our students deserve? No. It is not the business of American pedagogy to base its curricula on what are imagined to be students' fears. It is not the business of American education to encourage any kind of unreasoning fear.

Nor is it proper to use American classrooms for "creating a

grassroots network of educator activists," as Educators for Social Responsibility, one of the most aggressive advocates of peace curricula, has described its goal. In an educational system with a limited but difficult mission—to teach basic knowledge, basic skills, and the values necessary for democratic citizenship—there is no room for propaganda or political activism. Yet peace studies are the creation of a *political* movement that seeks at least a nuclear "freeze," at most, unilateral disarmament. It is a movement that has designed lesson plans urging students to petition their elected representatives about the threat of nuclear war. It has called on our schools to institute "infusion workshops" in which teachers set aside entire days "to grow in enthusiasm for justice and peace education." This is not education; this is indoctrination, and much of it is just what it sounds like—a perfectly preserved fossil of 1960s-style activism.

Other Education Fantasies

Another legacy from the "Age of Aquarius" that has been enshrined in too many of our social studies curricula is a disturbing anti-rational bias. Curriculum guides for what is known as "global education" are shot through with calls for "raised consciousness," for students and teachers to view themselves "as passengers on a small cosmic spaceship," and for classroom activities involving "intuiting," "imaging," or "visioning" a "preferred future." Two proponents of such curricula have offered a candid caution: "These exercises may seem dangerous to your logical thought patterns. For best results, suspend your judging skills and prepare to accept ideas that seem silly and/or impractical." Well, if we are going to give up critical judgment, we had better give up genuine education altogether.

Then there is the grandest shibboleth of them all—the notion that we must never judge other societies or other political systems. Indeed, the habit of making such judgments is alleged to be a major failing of the traditional way of teaching about the world. As guidelines published by the National Council for the Social Studies put it, the traditional social studies curriculum "reflected the biases of the white middle class" and distorted non-Western cultures. American teaching, these guidelines complain, "concealed the diversity of the social world . . . [and] reinforced cultural bias and ethnocentricity." But it is *this* society, after all, in its freedom, its scholarship, and its tolerance, that has established a matchless record for the willingness to provide an open and sympathetic hearing for diverse ideas. It is *this* country that sends open-minded social scientists and cultural anthropologists to study even exceedingly close-minded, ethnocentric societies abroad. We have benefited from those studies; we are committed to learning from the customs and the values of other cultures and other societies; and we have an historically unprecedented appetite for self-scrutiny and self-criticism.

A Recipe For Teaching

A rational, realistic, and open-minded approach to international politics is possible for American high schools. But we do not have to teach the subject as diluted cultural anthropology, arguing in effect that all the world's governments are the same because all their people drink water and breathe air, and that no society's practices are better than any other's. To put the matter succinctly, you cannot put liberal democracy and Communism equally together on any moral map of the world. Wishes will not replace the fact that American citizens share almost nothing of political life with the subjects of a totalitarian government.

That American textbooks should eschew xenophobia is obvious. They should clearly and factually teach our children what they need to know about other countries and cultures. But openness and honesty requires as well the acknowledgement that not all systems are humane, decent, or legitimate. It is not ethnocentrism but—to the contrary—an honest commitment to universal criteria of judgment that requires us to discriminate among the societies of the world. All men are created equal but all political and social systems are not. By universal criteria, some are simply awful. Their people live in misery, are oppressed by their governments, and are denied their dignity. Just as we do not shrink from telling the truth about American slavery, let us tell the more horrible truth about the extermination of tens of millions of people in Stalin's Russia. School textbook publishers or teachers may approve or disapprove of particular American foreign policies. As free citizens, they are entitled to their opinions. But as educators, their obligation is to tell the truth and the facts.

Americans instinctively abhor governments that attempt to enforce intellectual conformity on their people. But we nonetheless know certain things with certainty. We therefore cannot abdicate our responsibility to inform our children about the world around them. Too many of our textbooks teach only that Communism is an ideology that preaches common ownership of property and wealth, that Communist nations such as the Soviet Union have reduced illiteracy, and that, as one textbook asserts, "equality for women in the USSR is a reality. . . . They may marry or vote when they are eighteen." Vote? Vote for what?

By contrast, how should our high school students be taught international politics? What is "global education," properly understood? The answers are that students should learn geography and foreign languages, some foreign literature, and a lot of European history. They should be familiar with Western civilization's religious traditions, and with the central place of religion in the lives of its peoples. They should be aware of totalitarianism's ghastly contempt for the triumph of religious liberty in the West, and of the unnatural replacement of God by man and state under Communism. Students should learn about the Greeks, and about the Romans; about feudalism, the Magna Carta, the Renaissance, and the Enlightenment; about the French Revolution, the Industrial Revolution, and the Russian Revolution; about World War I and World War II.

Our children should know first about themselves, about American literature, American history, American democracy. What are democracy's basic elements and fundamental ideas, the values necessary to sustain it, and the conditions for its success or failure? Then they should know about totalitarian regimes. What are their ideological roots? How have they acted in the past and how do they act in the present toward their own people and toward other nations? Our students should also know about the gradations of social, political, and economic arrangements in today's world between the few islands of the free and democratic and the vast encroaching ocean of the unfree and the despotic.

Finally, our high school students should learn about the key events of the last forty years that have made relations between the United States and the Soviet Union what they are. What happened at Yalta and why was Churchill so agitated there? What was the Marshall Plan? What is containment? What happened in East Germany, Hungary, Czechoslovakia, and Cuba? What is happening in Poland, Afghanistan, and Nicaragua today? And, yes, what was Vietnam? Tangentially, our students should learn about the meaning of "human rights." In 1982, the National Council for the Social Studies published a booklet entitled "International Human Rights, Society, and the Schools." It was designed to help social studies teachers teach about human rights. But the booklet was written on "a small cosmic spaceship" called global education—a place, as we have seen, where judgment is suspended. It said that there is more than one human rights tradition: "In Western Europe and the United States civil rights and political rights such as freedom of speech, voting, and due process are of prime concern. In Eastern European countries, economic rights such as the right to work, to form trade unions, to strike, and to take vacations are considered essential. . . . The rights which are deemed most important depend upon the social, economic, legal, and political traditions of the people."

This won't do, and not just because Eastern European rights to form unions and strike are an hallucination. The Soviet Union's constitution grants its citizens a long list of rights, but they cannot be exercised. Our children should read the Soviet Constitution; but they should recognize the difference between what exists on paper and Soviet reality; they should understand that every society falls short of its noblest ambitions, but must be able to discern whether the ambitions themselves are real or merely hypocritical—in short, are they a lie?

The best "global education" for American students is the

truth—the truth about ourselves, our political culture, and our intellectual legacy, and the truth about the world in all its friendly and hostile aspects, for all its good and all its evil. Though our scholars and statesmen are forever adding to its finer contours, most of us are agreed about what the bulk of that truth looks like. It is high time that we began making sure our children can see it too.

In this society, and in other free societies, we urge that our students be told the truth. We urge it in good faith. Think about that. It is an important measure of the state of the world. Can my counterparts from unfree societies, in good faith, urge the truth for students? Ask them. You will hear the silence.*

---

*Some time after Secretary Bennett wrote this paper, the Soviet Union began its experiment with *glasnost* (openness) and *perestroika* (reconstruction). At the end of the school year 1988, all history examinations in Soviet schools were cancelled, because, in the words of *Pravda,* the students had been using textbooks based on *lies.—Ed.*

International Politics and Global Education

MAURICE A. EAST

ANYONE INVOLVED IN teaching international politics should be convinced of the need for a greater understanding and knowledge of international affairs and foreign cultures. There is no need to waste time "identifying the problem"; it is the solutions that we must define. And we must do so creatively and realistically. We must also work within the system, for the curriculum cannot be expanded indefinitely. We must work with the teachers who are currently in the classroom, recognizing their strengths and limitations, and at the same time exploring new ways of training teachers, organizing schools, and improving incentives for outstanding instruction. We must also work within our communities. A school reflects its community, and our communities are becoming increasingly aware of international affairs.

If we are to teach international politics in high schools, it is important to distinguish between "international affairs," "global studies," and "international politics." The growth of international studies education over the last twenty years indicates that we need to place more emphasis on the *political dynamics* at work throughout the world. It is crucial to reassert the fundamental role of *power*—a concept that has sometimes been shunted aside—in international politics.

Maurice A. East became dean of the George Washington School of Public and International Affairs in January 1985. His degrees are from Colgate University and Princeton; he has been a Fulbright Scholar and Fulbright Lecturer in Norway. He has published widely in scholarly journals and written several books, including *Creon: A Foreign Events Data Set* and *Why Nations Act: Theoretical Perspectives for Comparative Foreign Policy Studies*.

11

We must also make clear that international conflict is neither abnormal nor unusual. International conflicts are inevitable. Our task as educators is to explore the historical causes of conflicts. We must also focus on general international trends and ideological distinctions, such as the balance of military forces, the various religious movements, the growth and effectiveness of international organizations, and changing international economic patterns.

We must also teach in the context of *American* institutions, and evaluate our unique national experience in contradistinction to the experience of other parts of the world. This will require that school systems take more interest in teaching about American institutions, values, and experiences.

Power, force, and war are not, of course, the totality of international affairs. Given the global complexities and the extreme risks we now face, it is urgent that we learn more about how to control international conflicts. What institutions, for example, might be built that could effectively deal with international problems? And perhaps more important, what means are available for mobilizing the resources of nations and organizations to resolve transnational problems? It is becoming painfully clear that no nation—not even the United States—can accomplish these tasks alone.

The Global Studies Controversy

A great deal of controversy has arisen concerning global studies. The concept of global studies became prominent in the late 1960s and was adopted by virtually all of the major projects in international studies education. Although for the past fifteen years the global studies curriculum has been hailed by the majority of educators, the phrase today carries the weight of both the best and the worst in the program. Many of us in the international studies field believe the embittered controversy that has sprung up—a dispute that only serves to dissipate the energy and resources of educators—can be laid at the door of a tiny number of people working under its rubric. These people have espoused a radical policy that supplants the importance of the nation and loyalty to the nation with supranational organizations, global concepts, and world-encompassing loyalties. This ideology is not shared by the vast majority of those who are striving to enhance international education in the schools. Most professionals are concerned with geography, language studies, the appreciation of diverse cultures, the resolution of conflicts, economic independence, and power as it affects international affairs.

A more recent development is encouraging, however. Good educators in the international field (they are many) are gathering under a single rubric, the Alliance for Education in Global and International Studies (AEGIS). The word "global" in the organization's title may be politically unfortunate, but efforts to improve global education must transcend politicized labels and phrases. If we are to be responsible educational critics and reformers, if we wish to pass judgment on organizations or texts, we should begin by considering the objectives and values in the instructional materials. Whether as citizens, parents, or school critics, we must bear the burden of discriminating analysis before we engage in a general condemnation of all who have engaged in the movement for global education.

The Realities of Foreign Policy Making

JOHN P. ROCHE

MY INSISTENCE ON being realistic in foreign policy stems from my two years in President Lyndon Johnson's White House and from other years as an historian of the early republic. In this perspective, the Irangate crisis, for example, seems to be pretty small-time stuff. The headlines that reflect major historical events read like this: "President Fires Secretary of State, Allegedly Called Him 'Enemy Mole.' " In August 1795 President George Washington thus accused his secretary of state, Edmund Randolph, of being an agent of the French. The French minister, Fouche, had in effect reported to his authorities: "I've got Randolph in a suitcase; I'm bribing him." The British had intercepted this communication and Sir William Eden, chief of the British intelligence service, passed the documents on to some of Alexander Hamilton's stooges. They told Washington the story; Washington called in Randolph and summarily fired him.

Think of the circus our press would have with this chain of events today: "Former Secretary of State Thomas Jefferson, like Randolph a former governor of Virginia, refused to comment, but his intimate friend, Representative James Madison, is said to have told Judge Spencer Roane that, 'Ever since the Constitutional Convention, I have never figured out what side of the street Ed was working.' Colonel Hamilton, reached in New

John P. Roche is the John M. Olin Professor of American civilization and foreign affairs at the Fletcher School of Law and Diplomacy, Tufts University. He is the author and editor of many books dealing with domestic and foreign politics, and has published many scholarly articles as well as some 400 reviews and columns in popular journals.

York, said cryptically, 'Ed couldn't have done it on his own. Of course, he is a cousin of Mr. Jefferson's and the latter, a very fine man, has a weakness for the French.' "

Consider another episode of the early republic. I can just see the *Washington Post* headline: "Vice President Aaron Burr Kills Former Treasury Secretary Hamilton In Jersey Gunfight." The year was 1804, and those were lively times, but the investigative press was not yet in its prime.

The Classroom Challenge

It is with this historic perspective in mind that we must diagnose the challenges of teaching international politics. The subject demands attention at every level of education. The sad fact is that even first-class students from leading institutions arrive at various colleges and graduate schools—including professional schools of international affairs—as historical innocents. They probably know a great deal more about sex than I ever knew at their age and a great deal more about some other things that I'm glad I know nothing about. But when it comes to the Hobbesian world out there, they are remarkably unaware.

This problem has concerned me for many years. The cause, I think, is that international politics is an educational rogue elephant. History, politics, cultural anthropology, social science, and other formal subjects are, of course, essential to an understanding of the world. But they are not sufficient to understand, let alone teach, international politics. Moreover, recent efforts to make foreign policy into a subdivision of theology have tended to generate inappropriate other-worldly attitudes in elite circles, notably the media.

For example, a journalist recently asked me why Israel wants to help Iran in its war with Iraq. My reply was "the Israelis probably hope the Iran/Iraq war will go on forever, so they want the Iranians to be able to hold up their own end." The journalist was scandalized. "The Israelis want war?" he asked. "No, of course they don't want war," I responded, "but since Iraq is still at war with Israel—it never signed the cease-fire agreement in 1948—they do not want 800,000 Soviet-equipped Iraqi soldiers fighting Israelis. They'd much rather have them fighting Iranians.'' The journalist immediately accused me of being a cynic.

A trained diagnostician, of course, should not be overly pious; in any case, there is a vast difference between piety and morality. It is not the best moral approach to apartheid in South Africa, for example, to encourage a slaughter there, yet many pious people seem to think it would be morally uplifting. As an old soldier I can tell you that such people haven't checked the Pretoria government's arsenal. And if war were to occur in South Africa, it is not the pious who would be spilling their own blood. At best they might erect a monument to the dead blacks as some sort of meaningful existential statement.

The teaching of international politics is *sui generis*. Simulation exercises and case studies can be useful, but such instructional techniques are akin to using the game of "Monopoly" to prepare real estate agents for major deals.

Making Policy Decisions

After I left the White House, I was often asked how people could be trained to exercise power correctly. I would almost burst out laughing. I could only reply that learning to exercise power with integrity is like learning how to die with dignity. But the metaphor is inadequate because it is one thing to be a kibitzer, but something quite different—and to me quite terrifying—to be in a position of personal responsibility.

Take the following. The date is the last week of May 1967 and the Middle East is heating up. It is about three in the morning in the Situation Room in the basement of the White House. The problem is that an attack carrier, the U.S.S. *Intrepid,* is heading from Newport News to the South China Sea and must proceed through the Suez Canal with a destroyer escort. The *Intrepid* is off Malta and the question was: should the ship go on through the canal, or should she be turned around and sent on a long detour around the Cape of Good Hope?

Present were President Johnson, Walt Rostow, and about four or five others. Rostow laid out the options—through the Suez

Canal or around the Cape. The president said he had discussed the matter thoroughly, but he wanted one more briefing before making his decision. So each of us offered his views.

The possible consequences were extremely serious. On the one hand, Gamal Abdel Nasser, the president of Egypt, might sink the *Intrepid;* or he might simply sink a cement barge in front of her and a cement barge behind her, and the *Intrepid* would be there right now as the Suez Hilton. On the other hand, if we turned the ship around, our decision might signal to Nasser that we were afraid of him. So the president asked everybody around the table, "What do you think?" I said, "Push her through." After everyone had said his piece, the president got up, said, "Thank you, friends," and left.

Half an hour later the *Intrepid* was on course for the canal. The president made that decision, I did not. But I could not sleep for three nights. In fact, I had the National Military Command Center call me every three hours to tell me what was going on. Finally, on June 1 the *Intrepid* cleared Suez.

Now, the problem we all face in considering "the teaching of international politics" is that all the history and social science courses in existence could not prepare anyone for dealing with the kind of situation just described.

Another illustration might be worthwhile. It, too, is from the summer of 1967. Eugene Rostow, who was then undersecretary of state for political affairs, asked me if the president would be interested in being briefed on the historical background of the Middle Eastern conflict. The president said yes; he hated to read doctoral dissertations, but he loved to listen to good, sharp presentations. So on the appointed day, two senior foreign service officers, the president, and I met in the cabinet room. Each of the foreign service officers gave a splendid half-hour synopsis.

The president was absorbed because he had a computer-like memory. He thanked the officers and then said, "Gentlemen, before you leave I'd like to ask you a question." "You," turning to one of them, "have given me a splendid summary of Zionism and Israeli development, and," turning to the other, "you told me a lot of very interesting things about the Arabs. Now I have a problem with those folks; what does your history tell me to do?'' Both replied that they weren't policymakers, and left.

Back at the State Department, they said they'd been bullied! They did not understand the crucial point. President Johnson and other people involved in decision-making have inevitably to ask the question: "Here are two sets of facts. *Therefore, what do we do?*"

The Disinformation Trap

One more example of the kind of situation that does not fit into any conventional decision-making model. It occurred while I was at the White House trying to limit the political and military damage to the United States from phony North Vietnamese "peace offensives." Ho Chi Minh was the last of the Leninist old guard, and he had learned his lessons well. He played us like trout during the 1960s negotiations fiasco. He was able to do this because *we* wanted to negotiate. The North Vietnamese, on the other hand, looked upon "peace" negotiations as a weapon of war with which to wear down American morale.

These proceedings were as well rehearsed as a Russian ballet by Lenin. During the negotiations, the *Saturday Review* ran an editorial by Norman Cousins stating that he had learned from U.N. sources that Hanoi, through its consul general in Delhi, had told a top Indian official that the Communists would stop infiltrating South Vietnam if we stopped bombing North Vietnam. Now this deal had for years been part of our so-called San Antonio Formula. Cousins, however, said that the United States had refused even to recognize this offer, and chalked it up as another sign of Johnson's "war-loving"nature.

Now I happened to know Norman Cousins, and he was certainly no Communist sympathizer. So I thought the best response to his editorial would be to show him the top-secret file on the negotiations. The president approved, and Cousins came to my office to meet with Bill Jorden of the National Security staff. We showed Cousins numerous cables from our ambassador to India, Chester Bowles, an old friend and neighbor of Cousins's. We expected to convince Cousins that the North

Vietnam proposal was a fake. The cables proved that North Vietnam had leaked information about the "peace" offer to the press at the United Nations, and that neither Bowles nor anybody else could locate either the Indian or the North Vietnamese consul general. Bowles had tried to gain authoritative information on the offer but his efforts were in vain. *The cables were perfectly clear on this.* Cousins was very nice, read the entire file, and wrote another editorial in the *Saturday Review.* He was very nice again and thanked us for our courtesy, but he repeated his charge that an opportunity for a negotiated peace had been wantonly thrown away by the Johnson administration.

The only thing that Cousins hadn't read in my office was a supersecret two-page report under my blotter from the Central Intelligence Agency (CIA) saying that "a most reliable source at the United Nations" had told our agents that the "peace offer" was a disinformation ploy organized by the Soviet KGB. I could not show this report to Cousins, but I can tell you of it now because the source was the Soviet assistant secretary general, Arkady Shevchenko, who later defected to the United States and wrote a book that detailed the operation.

How can we teach students to understand this sort of tragedy-farce in a normal history or social science course?

In the more recent case of "Irangate," the United States faced a different situation—what I call "The Man Who Would Be King" phenomenon. There is a movie by that title based on Rudyard Kipling's story of a man who aspired to be king of an Asian country. Everything goes beautifully until the man is bitten and bleeds, thereby indicating that he is a man and not, as the people had believed, a god. In an instant, the whole web of authority that he has built is cut and unravels. In the case of "Irangate," the American media had been waiting for six years to unravel Reagan's web of authority, and they pounced. These are the kinds of complex situations that decision-makers face in international politics.

"Cultural Static"

Another consideration is what I call "cultural static." By that phrase I mean the difficulties that arise from differences in national perceptions or even in vocabulary. One particularly relevant example today is the American fondness for "compromise." In most of the world compromise is a dirty word. In Latin culture, if you speak of *"compromiso"* you're liable to find yourself looking down a gun because to be compromised is an insult to personal honor. The same is true in Persian culture. When the secretary general of the United Nations traveled to Iran during the hostage crisis of the late 1970s, he said on landing that he'd come "in search of a compromise." The Iranians promptly threw him out of the country because he had insulted their honor.

One of the classic instances of this happened during the Lansing-Ishii Agreement of 1917 between Secretary of State Robert Lansing and the Japanese. The Japanese wanted—and believed they had obtained—dominant power in the Shantung Peninsula of China. In drafting the agreement, however, nobody did a careful study of the difference between the English and Japanese versions. The idiograms called, roughly, for a Japanese "preponderant interest" in China; the English version granted the Japanese a "special interest" in China; but we signed both. This kind of cultural dissonance can come back to haunt you; in this case, it took six years to resolve.

Another illuminating instance appears in Gary Sick's fine book about Iran, *All Fall Down*. In 1978–79 a member of the secular democratic movement against the shah told Sick, who was then on the N.S.C. staff, that his friends were delighted that President Carter had repudiated the shah. This was news to Sick, who asked, "What's your evidence?" The man explained. "Well, when the shah came to the White House you permitted that riot, and the shah was crying from the tear gas used to break up the mob. That riot could not have happened without Carter's approval." The Iranians had interpreted the riot as an anti-shah signal sent by the White House.

A Study in Deception

In teaching international politics, props are sometimes useful. One prop that I am fond of using with graduate students is a

World War II spy film. It is about "Cicero," the code name of the Albanian valet to the ambassador to Turkey. The valet, who was a Nazi agent, photocopied top-secret documents in the embassy vault, including a set of plans for the Allied invasion of France. Eventually the Germans paid him in counterfeit British pounds and he ended up in a Brazilian jail. When the movie is over I ask the class, "Does anything in the movie ring false?" Only once has a student replied, "Yeah, there's something very funny about that. What were the plans for invading France doing in the safe of the British ambassador to Turkey?" The student who raised this question happened to be a retired CIA station chief.

That *is* the question; in fact, it was the very question that the *Abwehr,* the German foreign intelligence, raised at the time in Berlin. The *Abwehr* officials said, in effect, "Look, the documents wouldn't be there; they're a plant." But there was a fight going on inside Hitler's secret service operation, and the anti-*Abwehr* forces convinced Hitler that the document was authentic.

The document did not, in fact, concern Operation Overlord—the Allied landing at Normandy—but Operation Bodyguard, which was a simulated plan for an Allied invasion of Pas de Calais, led by General George S. Patton, whom Hitler was convinced was the only great American general. Patton was running around Scotland making speeches, which we broadcast via radio, and Hitler concluded that a great force was with Patton in Scotland and would spearhead the Allied assault on Nazi-occupied Europe.

We now know that German ambassador Franz Von Papen's first cables back to Berlin about the spy in the embassy were cracked by "Ultra," the British code breakers. And so the British had a grand time feeding disinformation to Von Papen. When D-Day arrived, the Fuhrer told Rommel, "Keep your armies north of the Seine. What's going on in Normandy is a feint intended to deceive us." Only three days after D-Day did Rommel finally go southwest—too late.

Decisions, Knowledge, and Ignorance

Given these grand complexities from recent history, what should we teach teachers of international politics? To establish some priorities among all the complexities, we must first undertake an intellectual division of labor. This is *not* to recommend anti-intellectualism, *not* to suggest that history is unimportant. History is vital. But while it is important to ask, is something true, we must take our students one step further and ask, "What does this something, this fact *mean?*" We must do this because the realities of politics, domestic as well as international, are concerned not so much with conclusions, as with *decisions*. Decisions are the stuff of international politics.

When an international crisis arises, policy analysts divide into two schools: one asks, "Why did it happen?" and the other asks, "What shall we do?" The first question is important, of course. Right now, for example, data is accumulating that in ten years may help us make sense of "Irangate." But people who are interested in conclusions can suffer from what Kierkegaard called "the paralysis of knowledge." That is, they assume that they cannot act until *all* the data is collected and all facts are known. Yet every day we all have to make very important decisions on the basis, if we're lucky, of 51 per cent of the evidence. This is certainly the case in the conduct of foreign affairs.

A young instructor once came to the Fletcher School and joined a discussion among several of my friends, including former ambassadors, about international affairs. He solemnly asked, "Did you think, when you were in government, that you had all the facts when you made a decision?" We thought he was joking; we were *always* short on facts. A shortage of facts certainly presents a problem, but decision-makers must decide: they cannot wait until somebody writes the definitive doctoral dissertation on Crisis X.

To some people, my suggestions may imply a certain anti-intellectualism. To these I refer the wisdom of Immanuel Kant, who observed, "It is often necessary to make a decision on the basis of knowledge sufficient for action but insufficient to satisfy the intellect." This is precisely the crucial distinction that must be emphasized in teaching about international politics. In addition to teaching students *why* certain events occurred, we must teach them to consider what a decision-maker had to *do*. We must emphasize *action,* even as we point out that inaction is often a prudent form of action. I happen to think, for example, that the only sensible U.S. policy toward Iran at the moment would be to wait for the political situation in Iran to stabilize or change. Such a policy might be called "purposeful inaction." It is not a policy of inaction undertaken simply as a means of avoiding a problem.

Witness a young assistant secretary who rushed into the Secretary of State Dean Rusk's office in the 1960s and blurted out, "Mr. Secretary, Mr. Secretary, there's been a coup in Bolivia!" To which Mr. Rusk replied with a quiet smile, "Don't just *do* something, *sit* there." Now, that's what I call "purposeful inaction."

"Purposeful inaction" is not indecision. More often than not, indecision is a wrong decision or action. Yet every day international policymakers have to make decisions—often on matters of life and death—on incomplete evidence, and if this fact distresses purist observers I can assure you that it also distresses those who have to make the monumental decisions.

Dean Rusk once said to me, when I was complaining to him about something or other, "Well, John, you can complain to me and I can complain to the president, but who is the president going to complain to?"

We must remember, then, that international politics is dominated more by perceptions than by scholarly determinations of objective truth. I have done a detailed analysis of how the Japanese attack on Pearl Harbor arose from Japan's total lack of understanding of American politics and culture, matched only by the failure by Americans to understand the Japanese mind. During a 1986 summer symposium for high school teachers, I discovered, for example, that only 5 per cent knew that Hitler had declared war on the United States on December 11, 1941 (not *vice versa*). One teacher said she hungered for factual material of this sort: "All we ever get is stuff about philosophy and the 'rational actor.' " Her teachers evidently assume that the individuals who precipitate wars and other international crises are rational actors.

May God deliver us from madmen of the Hitler ilk, but as the late Herman Kahn used to say, "No scenario about the future is more unlikely than a no-surprise scenario." President Johnson put it somewhat differently in one of his parables: "Down in one of the big bayous in Louisiana there's supposed to be very good fishing, so a lot of fancy fishing boats went out, but they came back without much of a haul. At the same time, an old feller with a beat-up, wooden boat, was going out in the morning and coming back at night with loads of fish. A brand new game warden assigned to this area got a little suspicious. Since nobody knew him yet, one day he asked this old boy, 'Can I go fishing with you?' The feller said, 'Sure, son, come on around about 4:30 tomorrow morning and we'll go out.' And off they went. They went way up the bayou and into a side section, and the old boy reached into a paper bag and pulled out a stick of dynamite, lit it, and threw it into the water. And whammo! He got out his nets and hauled in the dead fish. At this point, the young man pulled out his badge and said, 'Do you realize what you're doing is in violation of Chapter 76 of Title 18 of the U.S. . . . ?' At which point the old man reached in his bag, lit another stick, handed it to the kid and said, 'Son, do you want to talk law or do you want to fish?' "

This tale illustrates, alas, the situation that governments— particularly democratic governments—face more often than any of us would like to think. That is, a government is confronted by somebody who hands it a stick of dynamite and asks, "Do you want to fish or do you want to talk law?" No third option is offered.

The New Look in Social Studies

RICHARD H. WILSON

THE QUESTION FOR A curriculum supervisor such as myself is what, if anything, should high school social studies programs be doing about international politics? For example, should teachers be devoting time to current political debates in Washington, or should they focus instead on the Reformation, the Embargo of 1807, the New Deal, or any number of other significant issues of the past? My own answer to this fundamental question is that in general, not much class time should be spent on current issues in Washington, or on international affairs.

When people recommend that a greater emphasis be put on teaching international politics in the high school, two questions come to mind: (1) what should be done?, and (2) what can be done? In answer to the latter, teachers can do most things they are asked to do if they are given clear goals, explicit instructions, and the necessary resources. If tomorrow were to bring a strong national demand that the history and culture of Sri Lanka be taught, our teachers would see to it that students learned more than needed about Sri Lanka. So the issue about teaching international politics in our school narrows down to, what should be done?

My thoughts about the place of international politics in the high school curriculum derive from my experiences as both student and teacher. Recall for a moment your own high school social studies experience: "world history" was really "Euro-

Richard H. Wilson is coordinator of secondary social studies, Montgomery County Schools, Maryland. He has written several books—at elementary and secondary levels—dealing with American history. He teaches American history and education at the University of Maryland and George Washington University. He holds a doctorate from the University of Maryland.

pean history." All we learned about Latin America, for example, was that Cortez brought "God, Gold, and Glory" to Mexico, that the United States in 1823 pronounced a Monroe Doctrine to protect the Western Hemisphere from foreign interference, and that Franklin Delano Roosevelt developed a Good Neighbor Policy for Latin America. All we learned about Asia was that John Hay helped prevent China from being carved up by imperialist nations, that Commodore Perry "opened up" Japan and ushered it into the modern age, and that the Japanese attack on Pearl Harbor propelled us into World War II. Africa was important only through its European connections. This narrow view—only twenty years ago—was the traditional "world history" course that we now hear highly extolled in the rhetoric lamenting the "decline" of social studies education in public schools.

Today, then, our social studies teachers have a new responsibility. It is to teach with some degree of depth the histories of Latin America, Africa, and Asia—in addition to European history—all within a one-year course. How can we hope to include so varied a field into one course, the world history curriculum?

The same difficulty confronts schools in teaching American history. Again, recall your "American history" class of only a few years ago. It was a history of white men, usually "great" white men, doing great deeds. It was also a political history that reflected Herbert Baxter Adams's observation of a century ago that all history is past politics.

American history was primarily devoted to the good things that Americans have done since 1607—civilizing the Indians, creating a society in which "all men are created equal," thrashing the Mexicans, helping the Panamanians achieve independence, making the world "safe for democracy," and, if time permitted, stopping the spread of Communism. The course also strove to teach students about the values needed for living in a democratic society.

Teachers had to do all of this in a single year. Today by contrast, our students learn that history is not only political but economic and social in nature, and that not only great men, but ordinary men—and women—made this nation great. Again by contrast to the recent past, our American history curriculum now emphasizes that many ethnic groups contributed to the development of this nation, that Americans have not always been altruistic, and that some American ideals were long given only lip service. All of this, mind you, is to be taught in the same one-year American history course that we had twenty years ago. The inescapable conclusion is that there is simply no way to add to either the American history or world history curricula; indeed, both courses are already overloaded.

Curriculum Overload

The challenge presented by these realities is compounded in many states, such as Maryland, where our students are required to learn something about civics, and local and state government. We want our students not only to understand their individual rights and responsibilities, but to develop a sense of commitment to American values and democratic principles. We also want students to learn about the role of political parties and the election process, and to become involved personally in the political process by voting or writing to their elected officials. Teaching civics and government also involves probing the philosophical foundations of our political system as well as that of other systems. Naturally, such a course would require yet another year of study.

As a result, three of the four years of high school social studies are already taken up by courses that cover complex subjects. And there is near consensus that three years is insufficient to do justice to these three courses. In addition, social studies educators are currently being encouraged to add a separate year of studies for world geography and at least a semester for economics. And then there are the pressures from special interest groups who demand courses—or "minicourses"—in women's studies, psychology, religion, peace, nuclear issues, the environment, hunger, and the holocaust. These pressures may be well intended, but their single purpose is to get their pet concerns inserted into the public school's curriculum—our curriculum.

These, then, are the facts of life about the social studies curriculum in secondary schools. I doubt that many people, especially parents, realize how much has been added to the social studies education, which has undergone two decades of adjustment to the new realities of American society. If Americans were to face up to these new realities, they might agree that the high school social studies curriculum should do a few things well rather than attempt to do many things superficially. But they do not, and quick-fix proposals persist.

Essentials in International Politics

Few educators will deny that young people need to know about international politics. But what is to be learned, and how is it to be learned? There are complex answers to these questions. One involves the use of conferences. If, for example, a conference were to be held on the topic "Positioning International Politics in the Curriculum," I would encourage teachers to analyze the three traditional areas of curriculum: American history, world history, and civics and government. Teachers, that is, could highlight international politics in an explicit manner—the Congress of Berlin, for example, as pivotal to understanding modern African history. The Monroe Doctrine, the Embargo of 1807, and the 1986 bombing raid on Libya are other examples. By identifying a few outstanding examples of international politics in traditional settings, teachers would be able to help students grasp the significance of events, old and new.

What I resist, however, is the "presentism" implicit in the suggestion that students must be in command of current international politics. While it is true that the Danes devote 20 per cent of their history classes to the post-1945 period, it is also true that they do not undertake political analyses that might be embarrassing to their country. By comparison, in our social studies classrooms, we routinely cast a critical eye on American history.

A second answer to the questions of content and methodology involves helping students to reach reasonable conclusions about a wide range of issues and events. Teachers must do more than simply discuss issues with students. They must provide a framework within which students can learn on their own. When, for example, an important issue arises in New Caledonia, students should be able to make some sense of it.

Contemporary Issues Course

In Maryland's Montgomery County schools we provide a one-semester course in contemporary issues in grade ten. The curriculum is organized according to a well-known problem-solving process; teachers waste no time wondering how to teach. The course can cover any issue in the United States since 1960—such as the Cuban missile crisis, the Vietnam War, U.S.-Soviet relations, the Middle East, Watergate, the civil rights movement, nuclear arms, the federal deficit, to name a few. Each social studies department generally selects four to six issues per teacher. Teachers can also address one or two issues of particular interest to them or their students. Students are required to do four things: *identify* the issue; *describe* major elements of the issue (what were/are the events? who were/are the people?); *analyze* the approaches used to resolve the issue; *assess* the outcome and implications of the solutions that were applied. This procedure works nicely for the Cuban missile crisis, for example. In that situation, the crisis had a clear beginning; there were clear alternatives; the president chose the "right" solution; the policy worked and the United States won. Our teachers love to teach about the Cuban crisis first because it gives students a problem-solving structure that they can easily use.

There are excellent features of this course: (1) students spend an entire semester learning about recent American history; (2) students focus on issues that may still be vital; (3) students learn how to unravel the conflicting information available on an issue—that is, they are required to assume direct responsibility for their own learning; (4) students come face-to-face with controversy, with opposing viewpoints, and with conflicting facts and opinions; (5) students are so successful in the course that grades earned in contemporary issues are higher than in any other social studies course in our curriculum.

The negative aspect of the course is that many teachers dislike it and are uncomfortable teaching it. This is primarily because the course requires a great deal of work identifying and securing instructional materials. Many teachers, moreover, as well as and students, have difficulty with an inquiry approach to learning.

In sum, Montgomery County schools offer a course that might well be a model for the teaching of international politics. Our students are successful in the course and seem to like it. If I were asked to revise the social studies curriculum in grades nine through twelve, however, contemporary issues would not survive, because I would prefer to see more time spent doing a better job with American history, world history, and civics and government. I agree, that is, with social studies teachers who lament the superficiality of their present core courses. Social studies teachers simply cannot cover all related subjects well. If the community believes that some aspects of the curriculum are being slighted, someone else will have to assume responsibility for teaching them.

Secondary schools have already done a good deal more than colleges and universities to shed the do-your-own-thing approach to curricula that characterized the sixties and the seventies. It therefore behooves institutions of higher education to reinstitute the curriculum requirements that formerly complemented high school social studies education, to take on their share of the responsibility.

All of education has changed over the past twenty years. And while more is expected today of high school education than previously, the amount of time available for instruction has remained the same and in some cases has actually been reduced. We cannot, of course, return to the past. We must accept the new realities of today and help social studies education focus on the essential elements. International politics is one of those elements—but only one of many.

Note to p. 31: Whether the United States "won" the Cuban Missile Crisis is debatable. See Appendix D, p. 127.—*Ed.*

Trading States or Territorial States?

Jan L. Tucker

MOST EDUCATORS PROBABLY agree that there should be more teaching about contemporary international politics in our high schools. In contrast to the Danes, who devote at least 20 per cent of every history course to the post-World War II era, many history courses in our high schools barely cover the years up to World War II.

But while many educators agree on the need for more teaching about international politics and the contemporary world, they would probably heartily disagree about the content of instruction. I should like, as a social studies educator, to offer a comparatively new view of the content of international politics, one that highlights the concept of the trading state as formulated in *The Rise of the Trading State* by Richard Rosecrance, a professor of international and comparative politics at Cornell University.

A trading state is a government or nation that derives much of its security and well-being from participating in an interdependent global trading network. The trading state contrasts with the territorial state, which provides for its people through the control of territory. Japan and West Germany have been trading states since World War II; both were territorial states before the war.

Jan L. Tucker was president of the National Council for the Social Studies, and is professor of social studies at Florida International University, Miami. He directs the Global Awareness Program of Dade County Schools. He holds an M.A. and a Ph.D. from Indiana University, and has taught in junior and senior high schools and on the faculties of Indiana and Stanford Universities. For seven years Dr. Tucker served as N.C.S.S. representative on the U.S. National UNESCO Committee.

There are two reasons for the importance of the relatively recent concept of the trading state in teaching of international politics in the high schools. First, global economic interdependence is now a reality for the United States. Second, there is almost no reference to global economic interdependence in discussions about teaching international politics to high school students.

Yet 20 per cent of all jobs in the United States today are directly connected to international trade, compared to 7 per cent in 1974. This represents a 200 per cent increase in American jobs dependent upon international trade over the past decade. International trade now accounts for 25 per cent of our gross national product. More than seven thousand American corporations operate overseas, and they provide a third of all corporate profits in the United States.

Many foreign-owned corporations, moreover, have major production and distribution operations in the United States. States such as Ohio, Pennsylvania, and Tennessee compete for foreign corporate investment, and many states have created foreign-trade offices to secure benefits of the global economy for their citizens.

Forty per cent of our farmland produces food for export. A decline in Soviet consumption of wheat grown in Kansas, or in Chinese consumption of soybeans grown in Illinois, has important ramifications for foreign policy. The currently high unemployment rate in the port city of New Orleans, for example, is partly the result of a decline in agricultural exports. Thus the international economy increasingly affects the domestic economy.

Educational Implications

Although the United States does not depend upon the international economy to the same degree as Japan or West Germany, it is essential that any high school course in international politics include this increasingly important factor. International economic interdependence is, in fact, a cornerstone of the educational reform movement in this country.

Beginning in 1983 with *A Nation at Risk,* a report on the state of the nation's education, and continuing through the more recent reports of the Carnegie Forum and the American Association of State Colleges and Universities (AASCU), our education system has been challenged to meet the new realities and opportunities of our interdependent and competitive world. The Carnegie Forum report opened with a warning: "America's ability to compete in world markets is eroding. The productivity growth of our competitors outdistances our own. The capacity of our economy to provide a high standard of living for all our people is increasingly in doubt."

The AASCU report also emphasizes the close relationship between U.S. foreign policy and international understanding through education. In consequence, it urges a strong federal support of international education programs in both elementary and secondary education for three reasons: (1) to provide students with an international perspective that reflects the world in realistic social, political, cultural, and economic terms; (2) to provide students with international communication skills that will enable them to think, behave, and work effectively in a world of rapid change; and (3) to assist through research, technical assistance, study, and international service programs in the resolution of international problems with the same commitment that educational institutions now address domestic issues.

Because they annually graduate more than 50 per cent of all individuals certified to teach, AASCU institutions stressed the "need to concentrate on improving international education for future teachers in the nation's schools." The report specifically noted that "many social studies teachers today are ill-informed regarding world affairs." It might also have pointed out that 45 per cent of all social studies teachers teach only American history. Most of them were trained in that discipline; they were not trained to deal with contemporary international politics, for in colleges as well as high schools, many history courses end with World War II. Thus many social studies teachers are ill-equipped to keep pace with the rapidly changing world. They are equally unprepared to teach the new concepts needed to understand the contemporary world, such as the trading state.

Preparing Our Teachers

If American history courses are to be the vehicle for more emphasis on international politics, we will need massive retraining—with federal support—of our teachers. Otherwise, most teachers will continue to rely upon increasingly outmoded concepts, such as the territorial state. And this would be a grave error.

Teaching about international politics from a focus on the concept of the territorial state tends to foster a "know-your-enemy" approach that encourages chauvinism, stereotyping, and a dehumanization of the "other," whoever that "other" may be at the time. Success in modern war, for example, requires the enemy to be psychologically dehumanized. Modern warfare and propaganda have made this nightmare a reality for civilians and soldiers alike. The territorial state approach does not, of course, require such an aggressive program of instruction. But it does provide the context and prepares young minds for the possibility of conflict. An exaggerated, but real, example is the state-mandated instruction in Florida called Americanism vs. Communism. According to the state law, the course "shall lay particular emphasis upon the dangers of Communism, the ways to fight Communism, the evils of Communism, the fallacies of Communism, and the false doctrines of Communism." The course uses as a guide "the official reports of the House Committee on Un-American Activities and the Senate Internal Security Committee of the United States Congress."

By contrast, the trading-state approach to instruction would enable students to understand other nations and people, for it involves a fundamental cultural reciprocity. One cannot successfully trade on the international market without some knowledge of other cultures and languages. A trading state requires new knowledge and new skills, and most importantly, a new perception: the benefit of any one nation is intermeshed with the benefit of all nations.

If schools adopt trading-state assumptions, they can be encouraged to teach second and third languages, and to emphasize the positive benefits of cultural pluralism, cooperative behaviors, negotiation skills, and conflict resolution. These are necessary components of education in the trading-state model.

The new international economic realities must be built into the teaching of international politics, although we should not, of course, cease to study the territorial state.

My hope is that all educators will agree to increase courses on international politics in our high schools. The suggestion that it be incorporated into the American history course, perhaps on the Danish model, may be a good one. As we agree to greater emphasis, however, we need simultaneously to reexamine the content of international politics in the light of current and predictable global realities. The contrasting concepts of the trading state and the territorial state may be a good way to start.

Avoiding the "Isms"

Rose Lee Hayden

THE LATE FRENCH POET Paul Valéry once remarked, "the trouble with our times is that the future is not what it used to be." Valéry's observation has much to commend it as we move to get "back to the basics" in education, for clearly, the so-called basics have changed. We must, of course, strengthen and improve education, but we cannot afford to back into the future. Instead, as we teach our students about other peoples, cultures, and international politics, we must incorporate a variety of viewpoints and tolerate much ambiguity. Adversaries and allies alike of the United States will not accommodate themselves to "our way."

Along with this, it is important to emphasize that there is no such thing as a value-free social science. Somebody's supposed scientific truth may not be neutral, let alone scientific. We must, then, assist students to form values thoughtfully and intelligently, rather than belligerently. In training students for assessment and personal growth, moreover, absolutes and fundamentalisms are inappropriate. They must give way to balance, as well as to an intellectual accommodation of the untidy.

It is absurd that, in the process of promoting the values of democracy, some people are afraid to exercise democracy's greatest strength—diversity. At best, democracy is a decentralized process and, at times, a messy one. The consensus-building necessary to democratic government is often ideologically sloppy. It is, however, neither disloyal nor unpatriotic to point to one virtue of the democratic process, namely, its ability to avoid extremist solutions.

Rose Lee Hayden is president of the National Council on Foreign Language and International Studies. She received degrees from Cornell, Columbia, and Michigan State, where she taught. She has written a number of articles on international and Latin American affairs.

We certainly do not want students to fall into the pessimism that may be a disease of the spirit. Yet the human condition is often less than cheerful, and some trends are disquieting. Again, balance is necessary, and we must avoid replacing one misleading set of absolutes and choices with another. We must respect the marketplace of ideas and furnish students with a variety of approaches and data.

Unfortunately, in all the current literature about problems within the educational establishment, little attention is given to the student. How do we motivate students? We teachers talk about what is good for "them," but who are "they," what do "they" want, and why should "they" learn about the rest of the world? Students' minds must be excited as well as disciplined. Solid and balanced content—plus dedicated teachers—is one answer. We should never create a false boundary between the students' cognitive mastery of international issues and their affective desire to know more about distant places and different peoples; these should interact and reinforce one another—and they do.

In the area of foreign-language education, for example, enrollments are increasing. Forty states have insisted on a stronger language background before high school graduation, and seventy colleges and universities have reinstated some form of foreign-language requirement. A proficiency movement is, moreover, sweeping the country; "seat time" is no longer enough. It is no longer sufficient for a student to have taken two years of French. The student must now demonstrate ability to *use* the language as measured on a scale adapted from Foreign Service standards.

Sentimental Fallacy

Sentimentality—another pitfall in international studies—should not be exploited when portraying the human condition. Our mission as educators is to provide information with a humane outlook, but without misinterpretation. American students spend many more hours in front of a television set than they do reading about world affairs. Television images are vivid, come in snippets without context, and have a powerful effect. In warning against sentimentalization, I do not want to deny the worth of the "We Are the World" phenomenon. No one should be indifferent to starving children in Ethiopia. Yet a crucial dimension of the Ethiopian famine was not fully treated by the media, nor by those who strove to alleviate the suffering. The missing dimension is the extent to which the Ethiopian regime itself, in an attempt to settle political and tribal differences, deliberately exacerbated the hunger problem. The harsh reality is that a subtle form of genocide is one tactic some governments employ to smash ethnic and political opposition.

While educators have a responsibility not to use scare tactics in the classroom, the threat of starvation or of nuclear annihilation should not be treated in such a detached fashion as to separate these specters from their potential outcomes. Yet somewhere between despair and detachment there must be a middle range. Objectivity does not preclude debate, but embracing absolutes on either extreme of the political spectrum fosters prejudice, not enlightenment.

It is important to take a hard look at American foreign policy—how it works and how it does not work to the satisfaction of diverse interests and expectations. In this respect, the work of the Atlantic Council's Successor Generation Group is particularly instructive. Its outline of a basic set of values for democracies is balanced and even-handed; it is a promising initiative. Too many textbook publishers, in order to avoid ideological treatments of such controversial subjects as American foreign policy, have simply ignored much of our turbulent century, have "dumbed down" their books, or become neutral—the bland leading the blind.

Teaching Suggestions

Student voices are rarely heard in debates over curriculum. Yet if our students have no experience of civic as well as academic participation, they will not retain the information they are taught. We remember through practical experience as well as through formal learning. The two go hand in hand. We cannot teach students to jump straight to the operations center of the

White House, but we can help students develop a balanced judgment, make them want to participate—to speak out, to vote, and to belong to civic and other organizations.

The division of education into two kingdoms of grade levels (kindergarten through high school and postsecondary education) does not serve learning well. The learning process should overlap grades and levels alike. The current system, operating in fits and starts, does not allow students to unify their learning.

The reward system in education is often cited as another problem, for financial as well as social reasons. Little has been done in this area. Yet rewards can be many and varied. The National Council on Foreign Language and International Studies has, in fact, established several successful programs.

One such is the student town meeting. In conjunction with the Foreign Policy Association, high-level guest speakers give interviews to a panel of high school students and then answer audience questions. The first meeting was held in New York City and featured former Secretary of State Alexander Haig; the second was held in Atlanta with former President Jimmy Carter. Both meetings were televised and drew a student audience of over one thousand. They allowed students not only to reflect on, but to feel involved personally with the foreign-policy process in a unique way.

Another is called ICONS. This project in computer simulated translation and negotiation assists high school and university students to learn about North-South and East-West issues. Yet a third is INTEL-ED, located at the University of Pennsylvania. This project links classrooms via satellite and provides a means for U.S. students to have face-to-face discussions with students in Germany and Japan.

There are endless ways to arrange for students to participate in school-related and community-based internship programs involving foreign languages, distinct cultures, and international affairs. Travel and study abroad is not possible for all students, but overseas experiences generally "convert" the learner and change both his perspectives and career goals. As educators, there is much that we can do to assist our young people to travel within our own country, as well as abroad, and to obtain first-hand knowledge through doing as well as knowing.

Importance of Foreign-Language Instruction

Many observers claim that our schools have failed in foreign language instruction. In such policy discussions, we Americans often tend to concentrate on failures so as to bestir ourselves to action. Yet there are many promising practices going on across the country. We undoubtedly have the ability to multiply successes and improve educational realities.

There is plenty of humor in learning another language, a sort of blooper syndrome. A sign in front of a doctor's office in Rome reads: "Specialist in women and other diseases." In England, a sign in a small hotel reads: "We serve tea in a bag like mother." An English hospital informs, "Visiting hours: Two to a bed, and half an hour only." A colleague of mine who was traveling in Japan asked her hotel clerk for a wake-up call. A sweet voice next morning announced: "Your time has come!"

I have no doubt that *our* time has come to improve American competence in world affairs by strengthening our foreign language and international studies programs at all levels. We cannot allow our students to remain so ignorant that they are unable to locate France on a map. *Participating* in our democracy requires a higher level of global literacy and concern.

Let me end with a somewhat personal story. As a college junior, I lived overseas with a research team in the northeast of Brazil. I found myself in an isolated and very small community called Camacari. I was the lone American there, and I could not speak much Portuguese.

One day there was a knock at the door. It was the mayor of the town. He ushered me out to the town square where, it seemed, the whole town population had turned out. Where these people had obtained an American flag, I do not know, because many were even short of food. And where they came across a phonograph recording of the "Star-Spangled Banner" I will never know either. Though the town was too small for a priest, it had a loudspeaker. The mayor turned to me and told me that

the town was honoring me because it was the Fourth of July—
the day of America's independence. It was a day that had always
had significance for me, as a daughter of immigrants, yet it was
in the northeast of Brazil that I—the American who had forgotten the date—was being honored as a representative of our
system. I could not have received a better lesson in civics. I also
learned there that compassion as well as intelligence is needed
in understanding international affairs.

As a nation, we must educate a "successor generation." Just
as World War II led to the proceeds from the sales of military
equipment being transferred into a Fulbright program, and Sputnik resulted in Title VI of the National Defense Education Act
to support foreign-language and science, so increased competition from Toyota today is pressing us to become more knowledgeable and economically viable in a global system.

The place to bridge the gap between national needs and
individual motivation is in the classroom. It takes a long time to
become proficient in a language, even longer to sort out values
and organize oneself. My central theme is this: it is possible to
care about this country and to care about the world, it is possible
to be humane as well as skilled, to be smart and to be compas-
sionate. We can and must educate our young people to care
deeply about our democratic values and about the world in
which we live. To be so informed and involved is in itself a
patriotic act.

A State Project in International Studies

MICHAEL HARTOONIAN

THERE ARE MANY approaches to international studies education. The Wisconsin Department of Education, for its part,
has chosen to conduct a statewide program to improve international studies through the teaching of history, the social sciences, the humanities, and languages. The Wisconsin project,
we believe, offers valuable suggestions for all teachers and
school districts. Its framework rests upon the two pillars of
context and *content*.

The context in which the program exists consists of several
school districts that cooperate as a network in order to reinforce
one another and generate community support. Within the network, each grade level of education, kindergarten through grade
twelve, is addressed. The context design, however, goes beyond
the classroom to include several Wisconsin Area Study Centers,
including Africa, Southeast Asia, East Asia, and Latin America.
These centers provide us with a reservoir of expertise, a community of scholars, that improves the content of the courses.

This type of context also provides a better opportunity to
create *meaning,* particularly when students are given a full role
in the process. We believe in the notion reflected in T. S. Eliot's
poem "The Rock": "Where is the wisdom we have lost in

Michael Hartoonian, is supervisor of social studies education, Wisconsin Department of Public Instruction. Educated at Lawrence University and the University of Wisconsin-Madison, he began his teaching
career at the University of Wisconsin-Madison, where he now teaches
extension courses. He has written or edited numerous books, textbooks, and curriculum guides, among them the N.C.S.S. report *Re-
thinking Social Education: A Report of the National Wingspread
Conference on Social Studies Education* (1985).

knowledge? Where is the knowledge we have lost in information?'' In most international studies projects, there is an over-abundance of information, but little knowledge, and even less wisdom. Meaning, we believe, comes when we move away from the notion of information, particularly in isolated forms, and start making information connections and allowing children to create a base of knowledge from which they can make rational decisions.

With regard to the notion of "meaning making," I am suspicious of the attention given to personal rationality or what might be called a total focus upon the private person, and I am appalled by the lack of attention given to the public person. For without an understanding of the public good or public rationality, international studies programs make no sense. While personal rationality is a necessary condition, it is not a sufficient condition for maintaining the republic. On this point, I would recommend Alexis de Tocqueville's phrase, "self-interest properly understood." Properly understood self-interest is fundamentally the nurturing and care of the community. We must all remember that the fundamental purpose of the public schools is to nurture the republic. A great deal of meaning and public happiness can accrue from acting on that understanding. This should be one of the goals of international studies.

In addition to factual information and knowledge, our project is concerned with standards of aesthetics and ethics. We raise questions about both, and believe that beauty is related to other human needs. The humanities, including art, music, and language, play a large role in our program.

With regard to content, we first emphasize the concept of *perspective,* particularly with regard to time, place, and culture. We ask questions such as: do children have an opportunity to study people in different time periods—past, present, future? Do they study people in different places? What lands have students visited? The cultural perspective is studied throughout the program, and we try to stimulate students to define the meaning of "culture." Second, we are interested in investigating ideologies: why do people accept certain assumptions about people and society? Third, we are concerned with policymaking:

how can children become better policymakers with regard to the classroom, the school, the community, and as far as our imaginations can take us?

To enhance the program's content, we bring various academic areas together and look for a common denominator or a common language that will speak to them all. In the process, we have defined four elements that we want to bring into every teaching situation.

Aspects of Instruction

First, we want our students to be able to *conceptualize* reality from various points of view. Next, we want them to be able to deal with *causality, logic,* and *rationality.* By this we mean not only inductive and deductive logic in the traditional sense, but also the means by which people who are not familiar with our forms of rationality deal with cause-and-effect relationships. The notion of rationality, by the way, struck me when an Ojibwa (Indian) friend asked me, "When did American history end and on what island?" It's an intriguing question. My first inclination was to look into the future. But he said, "It ended in 1492 on some obscure island off Cuba. What you characters call 'American' history is an extension of European history with some African and Asian history mixed in." What kind of logic is he using? What does he understand as causality? We need to consider all such perspectives if we are to be honest in our teaching.

Third, we discuss the nature of knowledge in terms of *truth claims:* how do you deal with bias? with the nature of evidence? what does it mean to be a "developed" country? It is very interesting to hear students, even in the elementary grades, asking each other questions like, "What is your evidence?"

Fourth, we are concerned with the notion of *creative extensions:* how can children be creative in their stories? We encourage students to write, develop plays, and use creative dramatics, and regularly turn to the humanities for help in this.

I must say a word about *connections.* The human connection, we all know, needs to be maintained and nurtured. Connections are also important if we are to expect any professional growth.

Context, content, and connections between and among people are the criteria we are using to bring integrity to the international studies programs in Wisconsin. The network seems to be in place and one of the very interesting aspects of this activity is the amount of excitement created, not only in the five pilot schools, but in the school system as well. It is a start, and we hope it may become a model.

Global Education: An Ambiguous Innovation

RAYMOND ENGLISH

GLOBAL EDUCATION IS designed to equip American students and teachers to understand the twentieth-century world—a world of instant communication, supersonic travel, intercontinental missiles, and unprecedentedly complex international relations. Clearly, the time has come to expel the relics of isolationism and complacent indifference to the rest of the world from our classrooms and textbooks. While few persons would reject this proposition, two crucial questions remain at issue: (1) what should be the content of global education? and (2) what methods and curricular arrangements should be used?

As far as content is concerned, present global education materials tend to skirt around the hard realities of international politics—the struggles for power and ideological conflict. They dwell too much on a nonexistent future that bears little relation to the human predicament. History, for example, is conspicuously absent from many global education materials; so is political geography. Instead, students are required to discuss and hypothesize about imaginary situations and encouraged to state preferences and desirable future outcomes without adequate attention to realities, especially economic, psychological, and political facts. Teaching from some global education materials is like wearing earmuffs while conducting an orchestra.

Another troubling aspect of global education is its claim to a

Raymond English is a senior fellow at the Ethics and Public Policy Center. He was educated at Trinity College, Cambridge, and Harvard University. Formerly a professor of political science at Kenyon College, he became the director of the Social Science Program at the Education Research Council of America, whose textbook series, *Concepts and Inquiry,* was published by Allyn and Bacon.

49

new synthesis. A discussion of global education by a committee of the National Council for the Social Studies, for example, asserts that "Leaders in global education have over the years diligently attempted to define their field as constituting a new synthesis that goes far beyond" international relations and includes everything "on the global scene—individuals, multinational corporations, volunteer aid groups, nations, and non-governmental agencies."

This new synthesis, even if it were possible, could only be achieved through drastic oversimplification and distortion; nor are experts in pedagogy the appropriate researchers for the job. And even if they were, high school students can neither absorb so complicated an enterprise, nor relate it to the real world. The motives of human beings and political leaders remain as mixed, explosive, and potentially cruel as they have for thousands of years.

These inescapable facts point to the desirability of incorporating global education insights into required courses in the curriculum. The only realistic approach to understanding our complex and interdependent world is through the established academic disciplines: history, political science, geography, and international relations, with a smattering of anthropology and economics. Attempts to bypass these established highroads of knowledge and analysis lead only into swamplands of impressionism and arbitrariness.

Facts and Thought

A persistent trend in education—the "run before you can walk" theory—is prevalent in global education and has helped to lower academic achievement during recent decades. This theory stipulates that children must be taught to make decisions, select value systems, and engage in democratic self-government before they have acquired any basic knowledge and experience. Learning facts, however, is not only compatible with thinking; it is essential to sound thought.

Proponents of global education constantly allude to the need to teach "critical thinking," and "higher-order thinking."

Rather than imbibing past wisdom, the students must forever be making choices based on their inexperience and ignorance. Patriotism, for example, is pitted against internationalism, whereas in truth, patriotism is not the antithesis to internationalism. In the same vein, protectionism versus free trade is a complex issue, not easily given to simplistic choice or solution.

The global educator's emphasis on "critical thinking skills" and advanced "mental processes" sounds impressive. But these talents first involve the ability to read intelligently; to write and speak articulately, grammatically, and logically; and to know relevant facts. How can a critical thinker use his skill in global affairs if he knows nothing about the Monroe Doctrine, natural law, the balance of power, the Berlin airlift, Marxism-Leninism, cost-benefit analysis, and constitutionalism; or if he does not recognize Winston Churchill, Napoleon, Hitler, Julius Caesar, and Attila; or if he cannot locate Vietnam, Saudi Arabia, Istanbul, Zimbabwe, Nicaragua, or the Persian Gulf on a map?

Another notion enunciated in global education circles suggests that elementary and secondary schools are training "social surgeons who perform daily operations on the body politic." The self-assurance of such assertions reveals a somewhat eccentric view of both education and constitutional democracy. If it implied sustained and serious study of history, anthropology, languages, and geography, one could admire the educational vision. But the public schools are already under heavy criticism for failing to do the job they once did reasonably well—the job of providing basic and essential information and skills to their students. Educators do not improve their public image by dismissing basic and essential learning as beneath their dignity.

In short, a person must walk before he can run.

Incorporating the Vision

Let me conclude with a plea. Elementary and secondary education should concentrate on substantive knowledge and the acquisition of skills. The American Federation of Teachers put it succinctly in its 1987 manifesto *Education for Democracy:* "The kind of critical thinking we wish to encourage must rest on a solid base of factual knowledge . . . the central ideas, events, people, and works that have shaped our world, for good and ill, are not at all obsolete.''

Global education as a movement of independent reform has made some valuable contributions to education. It is time to incorporate its better features and insights into existing courses. This incorporation was the expressed intent of the founders of global education. If these things are done, the movement will have served an important purpose, and will escape the uncertainties and controversies that have recently marked it.

Peacekeeping in the Nuclear Age

KEITH B. PAYNE AND JILL COLEMAN

THE ISSUE OF peacekeeping in the nuclear age has caused great controversy in education. This is not surprising given the politicization of the issue of nuclear deterrence. The National Institute for Public Policy, however, with its impressive record of research in defense and foreign policy, has been able to develop balanced instructional materials on the subject.

It is essential, given their controversial nature, that the issues that spring from the very existence of nuclear weapons be handled as impartially as possible in the classroom; that is, neither a single interpretation of the nuclear debate nor any sort of advocacy should be permitted. Many existing curricula on nuclear weapons and nuclear war fail, unfortunately, to meet these criteria. A survey of the most widely used nuclear curricula indicates that much of the material provides a narrow interpretation of this complex subject and gives little attention to alternative perspectives.

There are a number of specific problems with the way nuclear

Keith B. Payne is director of research at the National Institute for Public Policy and teaches in the National Security Studies Program at Georgetown University. His books include *Nuclear Strategy: Flexibility and Stability* (1979), *Nuclear Deterrence in U.S.–Soviet Relations* (1981), *The Nuclear Freeze Controversy* (1983), *Laser Weapons in Space* (1984), *Strategic Defense: "Star Wars" in Perspective*.

Jill Coleman is a policy analyst specializing in arms control, strategic and tactical defense, and the moral dimension of nuclear strategy at the National Institute for Public Policy. She holds a B.A. in international relations from James Madison College at Michigan State University (1984), and an M.A. in national security studies from Georgetown University (1987). Her writings have appeared in journals including *Comparative Strategy, Defense Science,* and *Policy Review*.

issues are presented in many of these curricula. They generally focus attention on children's anxiety and fears about nuclear war while employing teaching methods that feed the intensity of these emotions. Through stories, exercises, and dialogues, they highlight the horrors of nuclear war and the threat that nuclear weapons pose to civilization.

The problem with this approach is that, by dwelling on children's emotions, "nuclear age" materials fail to provide students with the background knowledge they need to comprehend the political and historical context of nuclear issues. Without this context it is impossible to understand the nuclear debate. While a number of curricula, for example, discuss in great detail the human tragedy that resulted from the explosion of an atomic bomb over Hiroshima, they skirt the political and military rationale behind the United States' difficult decision to use atomic weapons to end World War II. By presenting the outcome of the war and other events of the nuclear age in highly charged psychological terms, while denying students the historical context, they distort the meaning and significance of these events. Students cannot therefore make a rational evaluation of the nuclear debate.

The approach employed in several of the curricula also tends to analyze the relationship between the United States and the Soviet Union from only a psychological perspective, ignoring their distinctive moral and political values. Existing curricula deprive the student of even the basic facts regarding the similarities and differences in Soviet and U.S. political values, institutions, national interests, and traditions—factors that influence national security policies and perceptions of nuclear issues. In addition, nuclear education curricula often fail to present a balanced or accurate view of the Soviet Union; the Soviet Union is either an aggressive power completely inimical to the United States, or it is no better and no worse, and no more aggressive than the United States. Both approaches are inaccurate in significant ways and can lead to misperceptions and stereotyping of the Soviet Union and the United States.

Another problem with many nuclear education materials is their tendency to present only one point of view about nuclear weapons, or to present several viewpoints while clearly endorsing one. In many cases, the groups that produced the curricula hold strong political positions on nuclear issues. Even worse, to increase student interest, some materials call upon students to undertake activities on behalf of a particular political viewpoint. While student involvement in public affairs should be encouraged, it is improper for instructional material to advocate activism in support of a specific policy view.

Guidelines for Nuclear Education

Educational programs should provide students with a clear and balanced presentation of nuclear issues. One of the goals should be to lay the groundwork in order to help students understand the basics of international relations and nuclear weapons. A second goal should be to help students analyze contemporary issues of war and peace and to realize that there is no single set of "right" answers to the nuclear question. Finally, a key goal of such a curriculum should be to teach students to assess various policy positions and make their own reasoned judgments. It is only by fulfilling these criteria that nuclear education curricula can prepare students to participate in the public policy process. Students must be educated, not indoctrinated.

In designing curricula that cover the major aspects of the nuclear debate, certain broad guidelines should be followed. The curriculum should: (1) provide students with multiple perspectives on basic nuclear concepts   not endorse one interpretation over another—and encourage students to make their own informed and cautious decisions; (2) present important events and policy developments in national security in their historical context; (3) devote attention to the political and cultural values of both the United States and the Soviet Union; (4) avoid a political bias or endorsement of a political agenda; (5) avoid the psychological or emotional impact of nuclear weapons; (6) integrate nuclear studies with traditional subjects such as history and social science rather than treat it as an independent discipline; (7) affirm the students' current and future participation in the democratic public policy process; and (8) present controversial issues in a fashion that is appropriate to the age and maturity of the students.

A Model Curriculum

The National Institute for Public Policy's project, *Peacekeeping in the Nuclear Age: Issues of War and Peace in International Relations,* is a curriculum intended to provide a basic understanding of nuclear issues at the high school level. The National Institute is a non-profit and non-partisan research center established in 1981 for the purpose of promoting public education in international relations and national security. Its scholars combine the necessary experience and expertise for this effort, including: university and/or high school teaching experience in history, international relations, and national security (several currently serve as adjunct professors at Georgetown University); direct participation in arms-control negotiations with the Soviet Union on strategic nuclear forces; participation at senior levels in the arms-control and defense-policy formulation process; career military service; and technical expertise in nuclear weapons.

Drawing on a broad range of professional expertise, the National Institute will develop a presentation appropriate to a given age group on the above subjects, focusing on international, political, diplomatic, military, and economic considerations. It will offer a balanced presentation of the different theories and interpretations of deterrence, arms control, and U.S.–Soviet relations. It will also stress the importance of understanding the historical context of significant events prior to and following World War II that have shaped the nuclear age.

The Institute will produce a balanced five- to seven-week curriculum that can be integrated with existing world history, U.S. history, and American government courses. Lesson segments (each comprising four to six individual class periods) will be able to stand alone so that, for example, a class that has thoroughly covered post-war history could move directly into consideration of nuclear weapons, arms control, deterrence, etc.

The curriculum will try to provide students with the necessary basic understanding of the vocabulary, concepts, and historical context of nuclear issues, and teach them to identify and analyze the various positions that constitute the public policy debate.

To ensure the integrity of the curriculum, a board of review has been established consisting of educational professionals and international affairs specialists. These individuals are all professionally involved in the field and represent a diverse spectrum of opinion regarding the nuclear debate. The purpose of the board is twofold: (1) to help ensure that each of the responsible positions in these complex issues is presented fairly and accurately; and (2) to help ensure that the curriculum is developed in cooperation with teachers.

The eight chapters are largely self-contained and each is suitable for approximately one week of instruction (with the exception of chapters three and four, which are designed to be combined with other units). The full course, therefore, should require between five to seven weeks. Each chapter identifies and explains alternative points of view associated with basic concepts of international relations. They conclude with suggested activities, exercises, questions, readings, and a bibliography.

There is more to peacekeeping than slogans and demonstrations. It needs work and faith, and above all, realism.

National Security in the Nuclear Age

JAMES E. HARF

T HE NATIONAL SECURITY in the Nuclear Age Project (NSNA)
based at Ohio State University's Mershon Center, pursues a
four-pronged strategy, the four "Ps"—philosophy, process, personnel, and products. With it, we hope to develop instructional
materials and training programs that will enable educators to
teach with authority about national security and to incorporate
concepts and facts about the nuclear age into their existing
curricula.

NSNA undertook the nuclear age project well aware of the
hurdles that it faced in attempting to include the subject of
national security in the schools. First, the study of international
politics in secondary schools is not an established part of the
curriculum. School boards, administrators, and teachers are
bombarded by individuals and groups who argue that if they do
not introduce someone's pet subject into the curriculum by the
next morning the educators will have failed in their responsibilities.

Second, schools have a crowded curriculum. There is too
much to teach and too little time, and there is very little room to
accommodate new fields of study, no matter how worthy.

Third, most teachers have a limited knowledge of national

James E. Harf is co-director of "National Security in the Nuclear
Age," and a professor of political science and assistant director for
development at the Mershon Center, Ohio State University. He received his Ph.D. in political science and an area certificate from the
Russian Institute at Indiana University. He is the co-author of nine
books on various aspects of international politics and studies, as well
as co-editor both of a six-book series on international business, and of
the Global Issues project (Duke University Press).

security studies. While I applaud the statement that we can learn much about the nuclear age by understanding Thucydides, most social studies teachers have not been trained to translate the world of Sparta and Athens into the world of the 1980s. The story of the ancient world *is* translatable, but teachers need guidance to impart the lessons of history to students so that they can better understand the issues of today. Hence, there is a need for in-service programs.

Fourth, instructional materials are inadequate. Textbooks give little attention, particularly in a conceptual and systematic manner, to important topics relevant to the nuclear age. If these topics are mentioned at all, it is only in an episodic and chronological manner. Consequently, many well-intentioned groups have tried to fill the void by developing materials, curricula, and other instructional aids, but all have so far been deficient in some fashion. Primarily, they fail to present the big picture of international affairs. A favorite theme in instructional materials is patterned on the movie *The Day After,* which depicted life in America after a nuclear attack; but few of these materials depict the day *before* a nuclear war. They thus fail to ask, how did we get into that situation? What happened? What was the international environment? Was there no arms control? Why was there no defense? Why did deterrence not work? The conceptual foundation for asking such questions is missing from available materials.

In addition, most materials on international politics pay little or no attention to the questions of scope and sequence, or to timing—when, that is, the teacher should use the material. Nor is there any recognition that, contrary to popular belief, the social studies curriculum is not infinitely expandable, that it cannot absorb everything. Finally, there is no financial support for the groups that are capable of correcting these curricular deficiencies.

We believe that social studies education is important in a democracy because it assists students to participate effectively as knowledgeable, responsible citizens. This means that students must understand public-policy issues, learn about traditional values, and handle ideas wisely in order to deal with these issues effectively. One of the most pressing of these public-policy issues today is national and global security.

Criteria for Project Materials

These are some of the problems that the NSNA has pin-pointed. As a result, we established a set of criteria to guide the development of instructional materials.

First, the material that we develop for teachers or for students should be *balanced and free of advocacy*. Public education should not try to advance explicitly any one point of view regarding national security topics. Further, where appropriate, such materials should explain various perspectives on national security issues. This is a difficult task, but not impossible.

Second, the material should be anchored in a *conceptual foundation* drawn from university-based research in national security studies. Teachers need some understanding of the conceptual foundation of a subject in order to teach it with confidence. Teachers are a creative group. They can do many great and different things, such as using this conceptual foundation in a variety of educational environments.

Third, we think it critical that there be greater interaction between *two kinds of specialists:* national security research scholars and social studies educators. Most of the projects that we have scrutinized suffered from the failure to call upon one or the other; we have brought the two together. Development of the NSNA instructional materials has involved teachers, social studies supervisors, and state social studies coordinators working cooperatively with a multidisciplinary group consisting of political scientists, economists, geographers, historians, university social studies coordinators, and national security specialists.

Fourth, education about national security should be *infused into the curriculum* rather than grafted on as a new element. Revision of the entire curriculum to address national security issues is neither necessary nor appropriate. While teaching Thucydides, for example, the teacher ought to draw parallels between ancient Greece and challenges of the nuclear age. It is not necessary to delay teaching about global politics until the course reaches the post-1945 era. There are thousands of places throughout the existing curriculum where nuclear age links can be forged without changing basic structure.

Fifth, teachers must be *adequately trained* before introducing discussion of the nuclear age. This training must include pedagogical methods, of course, but also instruction in the content of the subject and some understanding of student attitudes about nuclear energy. Naturally, there are start-up costs involved, but NSNA is trying to minimize them.

Sixth, *sufficient support materials* must be made available to the school libraries. Seventh, *important groups* in the community, including parents, must be involved. Their support, advice, and understanding must be sought and maintained. Eighth and last, teachers must be given the *full support* of school administrators and their board of education.

Process of Curriculum Development

The second "P" is the *process* we employed. In 1983, we asked the social studies coordinators of all fifty states to meet for a week: forty-three attended. The plan of action that emerged was similar to the one produced after two years spent at the state social studies meetings around the country. A particularly critical meeting took place at Wingspread, a retreat in Wisconsin, where groups as diverse as the Educators for Social Responsibility and the American Security Council agreed on a course of action. As a result, we began to work on helping social studies teachers introduce education on national security into the curricula.

Personnel

We established the set of guidelines already described and focused on the third "P"—personnel. From universities, we recruited researchers whose background indicated a lack of bias and an interest in pre-collegiate or undergraduate education. We then brought in experienced textbook writers, curriculum specialists, and other individuals skilled in both content and pedagogy. Everything was reviewed to ensure that it met our criteria.

Instructional Materials

The fourth "P" relates to the *products* we are developing. During the initial phase, we created four basic products. The first, which the state social studies coordinators told us was of the utmost importance, was a guidebook for the individual social studies teacher, *Essentials of National Security: A Conceptual Guidebook for Teachers*. It is organized around ten major themes that form a conceptual road map for the vast complexities of national securities studies. The themes are: premises for national and international security, conflict in the modern era, conflict management, strategy, arms competition and control, technology, policymaking, the economics of security, the military and society, and ethical issues. For each area we provide a narrative essay, a summary of issues, objectives, and annotated bibliographies for both teachers and students.

Our second product is a series of five books of lessons for high school teachers to use with their students. Each book contains about thirty lessons on national security topics that can be used to strengthen and complement existing high school courses. The books are: *American History and National Security, American Government and National Security, World History and National Security, Economics and National Security,* and *World Geography and National Security.*

A third product is a book published by the U.S. Department of Education's ERIC Clearinghouse on Social Studies/Social Science Education entitled *Teaching About National Security: Instructional Strategies and Lessons for High School Courses in History, Government, Geography, and Economics.* This book summarizes major themes in national security studies and describes eight instructional strategies. Each instructional strategy is illustrated by sample lessons from the five books of supplementary lessons developed by NSNA.

Our final product in this initial phase is an educational technology plan. We hope to develop a set of video cassettes to be disseminated throughout the states at no cost to departments of public instruction.

These few comments do not deal adequately with the subject. Yet surely we are all aware that succeeding generations must be rid of the misapprehensions surrounding the nuclear issue and learn to think in terms of national security.

Teaching About the United Nations

Juliana Geran Pilon

DURING THE YEARS that I taught college philosophy, I was fortunately able to teach Marxism from the original sources, Karl Marx, Friedrich Engels, and their successors. But toward the end of the course, there was neither the time nor the resources to explain Communism in practice. Working with theory alone, I tried to enable my students to make at least some sense of the complex and esoteric vocabulary used by Marx and his followers.

But that extra essential step was still missing—the explanation of what Marxist theory means in practice. Having lived in a Communist country (I emigrated with my family from Romania to the United States as a teenager), I know of Marxism in practice. My experience convinced me that I ought to instruct my students about Marxist concepts, such as the "dictatorship of the proletariat." This led me to become interested in the United Nations.

Since its inception, the United Nations has been a great dream—the dream of preventing war by providing a forum where people of many different cultural backgrounds and political systems could discuss and resolve their differences. I soon found

Juliana Geran Pilon is executive director of the National Forum Foundation. For seven years she was the senior policy analyst of the United Nations Assessment Project at the Heritage Foundation. Prior to joining the Heritage Foundation in 1981, Dr. Pilon, a native of Bucharest, Romania, was a visiting scholar and Earhart Fellow at the Hoover Institution at the Stanford University and a research fellow at the Institute for Humane Studies in Menlo Park, California. She is the author of *Notes From the Other Side of Night,* and earned a Ph.D. in philosophy from the University of Chicago.

that there was only one organization anywhere—in this country or elsewhere—that took a truly realistic and honest look at the United Nations. As a non-American—as someone who understands that there are other cultures with legitimate backgrounds and points of view—it was with special enthusiasm that I discovered the United Nations Assessment Program at the Heritage Foundation.

The "Model U.N." program used in high schools and colleges usually presents only the dream, the Utopian concept. Countries are depicted as talking with one another in an entirely rational manner. The reality of the United Nations is very different. One of the more striking realities is the extent of member-state violations of the U.N. Charter.

If we are to be honest about the possibility of authentic discussion among disparate countries and their governments, we must be candid about the ways in which that discussion is actually conducted. One of the principal stipulations of the U.N. Charter requires U.N. members to refrain from the threat or use of force against the territorial integrity or political independence of any state. We know, of course, that there have been numerous armed conflicts in the world and that the U.N. General Assembly has, on occasion, condemned them. Yet when the invasion of Afghanistan in 1979 was condemned by the United Nations, the Soviet Union was never singled out for censure by name. By contrast, the United States is routinely condemned by name in U.N. resolutions—doubly interesting to contemplate considering our idealism in international affairs and our enormous financial support of the United Nations.

More generally, the United Nations has so frequently ignored the Charter provision requiring that U.N. members refrain from the use of force that it has implicitly repudiated it. Consider, for example, the General Assembly's decision in 1975 to accept the Palestine Liberation Organization as a permanent official observer even though the PLO is dedicated to the destruction of a U.N. member state—Israel. Whatever one may think of the legitimate rights of the Palestinian people, and apart from the continuing conflict in the Middle East, the primary fact remains: Israel is a U.N. member state; therefore the United Nations' acceptance of the PLO as a permanent observer repudiates provisions of the organization's own charter.

The U.N. Charter is also routinely violated by the Soviet Union, which uses its U.N. employees for espionage purposes. In the summer of 1986, for example, Gennadi Zakharov, a Soviet scientist attached to the United Nations, was arrested for espionage. (In retaliation, the Soviet KGB picked up an American newspaper correspondent in Moscow on charges of "spying"; in due course he was exchanged for Zakharov.) The Zakharov arrest alerted U.S. authorities to the Soviets' abuse of diplomatic privilege and the bloated size of the Soviet staff at U.N. headquarters in New York. In response to American demands, that staff has since been considerably reduced.

The Zakharov case raises extremely important questions. Why has the West not taken a closer look at the United Nations? Why has the West failed to criticize violations of the U.N. Charter? Why has the West allowed foreign agents to spy under the guise of performing U.N. duties?

Double Standard and Moral Equivalence

Some of the answers are unsatisfactory. Most Americans do not want to abandon official dialogue with other countries. Other reasons, however, have more to do with apathy and even with ignorance and disinformation.

One of the most important findings of the Heritage Foundation project is the extent to which there is a *double standard* at the United Nations. Cuba, for example, has never been condemned by the United Nations for its outrageous human-rights violations, while El Salvador is routinely condemned for far lesser offenses. In addition, the United Nations has suppressed detailed evidence exposing Soviet atrocities in Afghanistan, including the torture of children ("toy bombs"), and of prisoners. The United Nations claimed rather lamely that the thirteen-page documentation of this evidence was excluded from all but the English language report in order to save printing costs. But the United Nations issued another document—no fewer than 105 pages—that contained two pages of pro-Soviet adulations; the rest of the 103 pages were nothing but signatures of students and professors from the Socialist Republic of Czechoslovakia. Apparently there was sufficient money to print that.

The hypocrisy of this double standard in U.N. resolutions is matched by the hypocrisy of its *moral equivalence*. Moral equivalence is the notion that all countries are ethically equal: some people kill here and some people kill there, and the reason is invariably laid to power politics. The two superpowers, the United States and the Soviet Union, are thus judged as equally moral and equally immoral. The Soviet invasion of Afghanistan for example, is held to be equivalent to the U.S. military action to oust Cuban troops from Grenada—no better, no worse.

Moral equivalence is one of the most dangerous and insidious notions disseminated by the United Nations. It is exploited to suppress the truth—that the Soviet Union is the perpetrator of the most frightening and far-reaching abuses of human rights in the world today.

Our work on the United Nations involves not only research, but continuous education of the public. We have been able to alert people to the fact that the United Nations, though intended as a noble experiment, spreads moral confusion. We offer publications on related topics such as Soviet exploitation of the United Nations, the U.N. campaign against Israel, U.N. attempts to regulate international economics, the World Health Organization, espionage, budgetary abuses, double standards, and peacekeeping.

Few of the realities of U.N. practices are being conveyed by our schools to the students. The study of international politics demands better.

A Critique of "Peace Education"

Thomas B. Smith

THE PEACE, DISARMAMENT, and "conflict resolution" instructional programs that have sprouted in recent years are politicizing the classroom to an extent probably never before experienced in this country. They are employed in practically all schools, and include such programs as *Choices,* a middle school course prepared jointly by the National Education Association (NEA) and the Union of Concerned Scientists; *Perspectives* and *Dialogue,* produced by Educators for Social Responsibility; and *Crossroads,* produced by the Jobs with Peace National Network.

The topics in these courses are chosen on an entirely political basis. Even when treating concrete historical events, they are slanted, selective, and episodic. All of these programs, for example, emphasize that the United States is the only country ever to have used nuclear weapons—the bombings of Hiroshima and Nagasaki in World War II. Yet none of the programs provides the background that brought about the United States' decision to use such weapons against Japan. There is practically no mention of the Japanese attack on Pearl Harbor, of the war in the Pacific, the Bataan death march, or the bloody island-by-island struggle to retake the Pacific. And there is no mention of the conventional bombing of Japan. I participated in the bomb-

Thomas B. Smith is director of the Center for Educational Integrity, and a member of the American Security Council Foundation. Educated at American International College and Boston University, he served in the Air Force in World War II, and later as a Soviet specialist in the Central Intelligence Agency. He spent nine years as a high school teacher and administrator. His major publications include: *The Essential CIA* (1975), *The Other Establishment* (1984), and *Educating for Disaster* (1985).

ings of Tokyo and the other large cities that were destroyed by high explosive and incendiary bombs and I can attest that more people were killed in one night of fire-bombing on Tokyo than died in Hiroshima. Had the war been allowed to continue, and had it become necessary for U.S. troops to invade Japan, it was projected that a million American servicemen and four million Japanese would have become casualties.

With this informational background, the dropping of the atomic bombs can be seen as a blessing to Americans and Japanese alike. With all its horror, it saved the lives of millions of people.

These special-interest courses also teach that the Soviets have no interest in war because of their sufferings and loss of life—20 million people—in World War II. But there is no mention of the millions of other people slain during the war, nor of the tremendous support given the Soviet Union by the United States—billions of dollars in equipment and food, and our sailors who died on the Murmansk run to support Soviet forces.

Further proof that the course materials advocate a political agenda is provided by the institutions with which these organizations so closely collaborate, such as the Coalition for a New Foreign and Military Policy, SANE, the American Friends Service Committee, and most of the other anti-defense groups in the United States.

The contents of the texts themselves are the main evidence of the courses' political attitudes. One single chapter suffices to reveal the bias. The programs, for example, employ some sophisticated psychological tactics admittedly aimed to train people in political activism, such as the high school programs prepared by the Educators for Social Responsibility.

There is nothing inherently wrong with teaching students how to work the levers of democracy, how to organize, deal with the media, approach a congressman, or even write letters to the president; these are all worthwhile endeavors. But it is quite another matter for our schools to encourage political activism to advance a particular ideology or policy.

Some of the organizations that prepare these courses clearly dislike the basic institutions of the United States. Their anti-

Americanism includes contempt for democracy, American traditions, and capitalism; it is not restricted to national security concerns.

What Should We Do?

With respect to international politics, given the proliferation of such course materials, how can we insure that the post-World War II period is properly taught in high schools? The answer, of course, is that school boards, superintendents, and principals must see to it. But parents and other concerned citizens should also monitor course materials. At the present time, texts and materials about issues related to nuclear energy and weapons are decidedly of the "peace education" variety. There are few materials that present the peace-through-strength view, and there are *no* textbooks on the subject.

Such materials do, however, exist. Many of them are free, and teachers should be using them. Though they are not standard textbooks, they include official publications of the State and Defense Departments whose facts and figures are reliable. The introductions and interpretations may reflect the view of a particular administration, but the figures speak for themselves. In addition, the Joint Chiefs of Staff issue an annual statement that contains a clear picture of the balance between Soviet and U.S. military forces.

There are other standard reference works that teachers should make a practice of using. Every year, for instance, the International Institute for Strategic Studies in London publishes *The Military Balance*. It lists figures of the armed forces of every country in the world with emphasis on the Soviet Union, the North Atlantic Treaty Organization (NATO), and the Warsaw Pact. It is compiled by an impartial group and used in many countries.

Can We Eliminate Demoralizing Instruction?

By contrast, many teachers who use the disarmament programs rely on sources that have a particular political bias, such as the Center for Defense Information, the American Friends Service Committee, and SANE. Since the organizations that produce these materials have a particular political slant, their materials reflect the bias. In many teaching programs, over 90 per cent of the resources listed have an antidefense point of view.

The same type of bias is promoted in "conflict resolution" programs in the elementary and middle grades. Conflict resolution courses, a recent development, have been made into a pseudo-science and are characterized by pseudo-scientific jargon. They employ some quite clever, apparently sophisticated, gaming devices in which children are asked to project themselves into all kinds of situations.

Far from instructional, these activities are psychologically manipulative, designed to have a particular effect on students' attitudes. The courses clearly undermine their sense of nationalism and patriotism. They make a positive evil out of every kind of competition, even sports. Their own version of games is of the noncompetitive sort. Such programs take valuable time away from core subjects that students are not learning adequately, as test scores from around the country show.

The same deficiencies are apparent in global education courses—a lack of solid instruction in history and the realities of international politics today. Instead, they teach students only that all people everywhere share the same human wants and needs, and that all countries have music and dance, that brotherly love conquers all. International affairs cannot be taught by sending our students on exchange tours and a sail down the Volga. We must give our students some detailed knowledge of other cultures and, above all, other languages. Unbelievably, even the Foreign Service no longer requires language proficiency, and American industry relies entirely on English or on paid foreign nationals overseas.

We must not allow our children's disinclination to master a difficult subject to determine the curriculum, whether it be foreign language or any other core subject. If international politics is to be taught at all, it must be grounded on facts and real skills.

The Historian-Filmmaker

PETER C. ROLLINS AND ROBERT T. BAIRD

MUCH OF THE DISCUSSION about teaching international politics in the high schools has focused on curriculum content. As a historian and filmmaker I have a different perspective.
In 1986, a Roper Poll revealed, for example, that 66 per cent of
Americans learn about international events through television.
Television and film dramatically combine eye-catching pictures
with *apparently* natural sound and *seemingly* authoritative nar-
ration. It is undeniable that these dynamic visual stories compete with classroom teachers for students' attention; given the
attraction of the medium, it is little wonder that students turn to
Dan Rather, Tom Brokaw, or Peter Jennings for information.

But what of *educational* television? Isn't it fair and historically
accurate? The answer, for the most part is yes, because educational television is well-researched and honest. The answer is
also partly no, as evidenced by several recent programs put on
by the Public Broadcasting System (PBS): the distorted studies
of Central American in *Guatemala: When the Mountains Trem-
ble* (1985); the biased view of U.S. military involvement in
Southeast Asia in *Vietnam: A Television History* (1983); and,
most recently, the diatribe against Western values in *The Afri-*

Peter C. Rollins is a professor of English and American studies at
Oklahoma State University and has made television production his
special field, having created four outstanding programs, including three
on *Television's Vietnam* (1983–85). Educated at Harvard, he has also
served as an officer in the Marines. His books include *Benjamin Lee
Whorf: Transcendental Linguist* (1980), *Hollywood as Historian* (1983),
and an annotated complete edition of *The Writings of Will Rogers*. He
has published more than twenty articles.

Robert T. Baird is a film scholar enrolled in the film and literature
program at Oklahoma State University. He has worked in Hollywood
on feature productions and has written about feature and documentary
films.

cans (1986). Because most television viewers assume that pictures do not lie, educators have great difficulty in teaching their students to recognize that much of what they see on television is made up of half-truths or plain falsehoods.

In the early 1970s, a new way of looking at documentary filmmaking emerged—what I call the "historian-filmmaker movement." A small collection of films has been produced representing an alternative approach to the popular visual media. In the journals *Film and History* and *The History Teacher,* spokesmen for the movement, such as Patrick Griffin, Richard Raack, and I, have called for a change in the current method of history and news presentation. Our historian-filmmaker productions have demonstrated that it is possible to produce films that enhance rather than hinder the teacher's role in the classroom and that develop students' "visual literacy skills." Though we stress the importance of training students to be critical viewers, we believe it is of paramount importance that our students also know the geographical location of, say, Mozambique and be able to "read" the images of that African country when they "see" it on their television sets.

The Problem of Distortion

My own interest in how television reports international politics was sparked during my years in graduate school after I had served as a Marine platoon commander in Vietnam. I was dismayed at the way the American soldier in Vietnam was being portrayed by the media. I decided to undertake a research project dealing with the 1950s television series about the U.S. Navy in World War II, *Victory at Sea,* and did some work with the series editor, Isaac Kleinerman.

On one occasion Kleinerman suggested that we focus on the episode about the battle for Leyte Gulf, which was not one of his better segments. When it was over, Kleinerman explained his reason for showing it. One of the challenges, he said, of putting together an historical documentary about that battle was that no film footage of it existed. I was amazed. He went on, "We had no film, so we put together this episode with footage from Hollywood feature films, from training films, and from combat footage taken from other naval battles. And they're still showing this program at the Naval War College!"

The revelation was traumatic because Kleinerman was obviously delighted at having fooled military experts. This led me to suspect that he was probably not alone in that dubious achievement, and that other creative film manipulators could cut and paste a bit of "reality" into Hollywood footage with all too believable results. The danger of bias is inherent in television and film because when fragments of sound and picture are assembled and reassembled, they inevitably represent the view of the filmmaker. Filmmakers assume that they can make their audience see and feel—and *believe*—anything.

A further danger is that historians are seldom consulted about historical films. Producers rarely purchase "properties" to use in connection with scripting. When, for example, the Project XX group at NBC set about to produce a film about the 1920s, they turned to Frederick Lewis Allen's book *Only Yesterday* (1931). With fiction footage presented as documentary images, the resultant film, *The Jazz Age*, confirmed current clichés about the period rather than providing new insights based on readily available documentary film sources. Allen's book has been criticized for its simplification of a complex era; *The Jazz Age* only further obscured the truth.

The Vietnam Program

A recent example of the misuse of the potentially beneficial film is the $6.5 million series by WGBH-TV of Boston entitled *Vietnam: A Television History*. A thirteen-hour survey of America's tragic loss in Vietnam, the program was assumed by most viewers to be based on Stanley Karnow's slight book, *Vietnam: A History* (1983). But in reality, Karnow's original simplification was even further simplified by the film, and finally trivialized. Like Allen's popular tract, Karnow's book carries little weight among historians. Even so, the television series was *not* produced by Stanley Karnow, but by seven independent producers hired by WGBH-TV. These producers had no training in history and knew little about Vietnam, instead, they relied upon their experience as college students during the 1960s, upon periodicals such as *The New York Review of Books,* and upon works of pseudo-scholarship such as Frances FitzGerald's *Fire in the Lake* (1972). Possessed of fervor where they lacked knowledge, these producers exploited Karnow's book, using it as merely a point of departure for their own views. Yet their series flourishes; it has been broadcast repeatedly over national television and is being heavily marketed to high schools and colleges by Films Incorporated. That such an inaccurate series is fast becoming a revered classroom authority about the Vietnam War is a sad commentary on the state of contemporary historical-filmmaking.

Critical Appraisals

Since the 1970s, journals such as *The History Teacher* and *Film and History* have carried articles by trained historians condemning this misuse of film and television. The essence of the criticism is twofold. First, the photojournalists who make many of the documentaries are not trained in history and so gravitate toward the popular interpretations of the events they depict. Inevitably, their "popular" interpretation reflects a distorted view. In the case of the Allen book on the twenties, the distortion came from interpreting the Great Depression of the 1930s as a form of retribution for the irresponsible preceding decade; in the case of the series on Vietnam, gross errors were guaranteed when WGBH-TV hired as producers antiwar activists of the 1960s who wished to justify their past.

Second, historians criticize the infrequent use of primary sources in most documentaries; in this case, the sources are films. Historians are trained to evaluate sources critically. Many items which might add flavor to historical analysis are rejected precisely because they are tainted by subjectivity. Historians are aware, for example, that many documents of the past are written by famous people who wish only to provide a flattering memorial of themselves and an unflattering picture of their enemies. But journalists and filmmakers seem to lack the historian's critical sensitivity. With an eye for the most dramatic picture or "scoop" interview, photojournalists leap at the opportunity to use highly suspect material. In addition, they face a deadline that tempts them to plunder, as cinematic producers did with the film footage used to depict the battle of Leyte Gulf.

In *The Jazz Age,* NBC borrowed extensively from *fiction* footage of the 1920s and 1930s and introduced it as *documentary* material—a clear violation of the historian's criteria for objective sources. In *Vietnam: A Television History,* WGBH producers had the unique opportunity of interviewing such Communist leaders as Le Duc Tho and Vo Nguyen Giap, but were so impressed at the "scoop," that the Communist leaders were soon in control of the interviews. Sadly, the producers presented the self-serving statements of these Communist officials as *primary* sources rather than as *secondary* sources that required careful evaluation. General Giap and a host of Communist officials were allowed to spout a party line that clearly conflicted with what historians know to be the facts. The journalists readily chose drama and impact over objectivity and insightfulness. Historians and those concerned with using film for classroom and general television audiences can only wring their hands with anguish that such practices not only are representative but are deemed the requisite for excellence in the industry.

The Passive Viewer

In addition to quarreling with existing methods of filmmaking, historian-filmmakers take a different approach to the viewer. Current news and documentary practices presume a *passive* viewer who must be constantly entertained with exciting pictures. This tempts producers to use the most powerful footage available, whatever it may be and however lacking in authority. Such an assumption also leads to the conviction that almost any viewer can be "tricked" because there is no limit to the viewer's gullibility.

The Soviets pioneered the study of film language. Shortly after the Russian Revolution they conducted laboratory experiments on how pictures could be employed—and exploited—to motivate an audience. Their most famous experiments showed that, because identical pictures can be interpreted differently, the *context* within which pictures are viewed gives meaning to a particular image, affects the ideas, thoughts, and feelings of the viewers. In a major experiment during the 1920s, for example, the Soviets photographed an actor's face with a neutral expression. They then presented this photograph in various sequences of film. In one case the picture of the actor was followed by a photograph of a gun; and most viewers concluded that the face belonged to a brave man defying a threat to his life. Then the sequence was reversed, the gun first, followed by the neutral face. The viewers concluded that the face belonged to a coward threatened by violence. The Soviets went further. They showed the same face after depicting a child in a bassinet; viewers saw a father looking tenderly at his child. And so on. Russian filmmakers rightly concluded that the *context* of a scene—not the scene itself—communicates meaning.

Education for "Visual Literacy"

One of the primary goals of the historian-filmmaker is to educate people to be visually literate viewers who can evaluate film as they would a printed essay.

Films produced by historians are designed to meet the standards of historical writing. In addition, they are primers of film language to acquaint students with the ways in which filmmakers assemble fragments of pictures and sounds to create their cinematic *interpretations* of the past. Students are of course encouraged to *enjoy* the film experience, but in a *critical* manner. After teaching such critical viewing in the classroom, I have been told by students that my course "ruined television" for them—by which they meant that they could no longer passively submit to the hypnotic power of the screen. They now realize that television is a type of text and that they are responsible for "reading" the text critically. They know, in other words, that they control their viewing; the viewing does not control them.

Film is potentially beneficial to education. It can serve as a primary historical material, and reveal events and personalities distant in time and space but relevant to understanding current international political conditions. In 1986, for instance, Americans did not know much about the Soviet occupation of Afghanistan because the major television networks had not turned their cameras in that direction. A similar void exists today about Angola, or about Soviet and Cuban activity in Nicaragua.

Suppression of Evidence

While working on a Vietnam documentary, I made an unusual discovery in the archives of the American Broadcasting Corporation (ABC). I found evidence that none of the three major American television networks had broadcast reports about the Hué massacre during the Vietnam War. Many scholars have assumed that there was, in fact, no actual film footage of the atrocity. But I discovered numerous reports about the massacre, including one that featured an on-site account by an ABC correspondent. Reflecting on how a report of the Hué massacre could have warned the United States about Communist plans for South Vietnam was a sobering experience. These visual records provided important evidence to contradict the false portrayal of the event by the WGBH series. (It should be noted that WGBH in 1982 had access to the same archive, but, as in 1968, the footage went unused.)

Audio-Visual Propaganda

Before the advent of television, the theatrical newsreel was an important form of documentary. Considerable research has been published in recent years relating how producers of The March of Time, Frontier Films, and other newsreels used their reports to sway theater audiences. The research showed how British newsreels depicted Hitler's rise to power in Germany in a manner that encouraged the British public to accept Prime Minister Neville Chamberlain's blighted peace agreement at Munich in 1938. During World War II, movie-maker Frank Capra, in his classic series Why We Fight, sought to inform Americans about the threat of fascism; the result was stirring propaganda for an arguably good cause, but Capra's films were so strident that they have not aged well.

The propagandistic and even mind-bending potential of audio-visual materials is intensified by television. Anyone who works in television production knows that the medium is interpretive: time constraints, the availability of footage, and the political persuasion of news reporters and network officials also contribute to shaping public opinion. Students in our schools need to be taught, by case-study tapes, how television operates as a medium in providing facts and informing opinions. Questions that students need to consider include: how does the format of television news contribute to the message? How does a news division operate? How do television personnel influence story selection and content? What are the ethics of television news?

Many filmmakers employ the powerful cinematic technique of *montage* to communicate messages. This dangerous technique in contemporary historical and political filmmaking is currently controlled by anti-American propagandists.

In the opening montage of the WGBH series on Vietnam, for example, though the narrator presents issues in a neutral manner, the pictures in the montage are arranged to portray American involvement in Southeast Asia as hypocritical, stupid, and wasteful. Thus, while a viewer hears the wise and fair words of the narrator, the subjective visual images quietly effect a quite different influence. A visually literate viewer would discern the intent behind such a subtle video message, but the passive viewer will swallow the message whole.

Need for Corrective Programs

In two documentaries on the Vietnam War that I produced, a primary goal was to educate Americans about the international consequences of the Communists' victory. U.S. Navy film footage of boat people was combined with commercial newsreel footage to convey the pain experienced by Vietnamese refugees. To heighten the effect of the tragic events, a musical refrain accompanied the reading of a poem in Vietnamese by a young boat refugee; the same poem was then read in English by

Charlton Heston. The purpose of the montage was to foster public understanding of the suffering experienced by millions of people after the United States' retreat from Vietnam, to rebut the WGBH series' view that there was no humanitarian purpose in America's defense of freedom in that tragic land.

Many veterans were disgusted by the way in which the ordinary American serviceman was portrayed by the WGBH series. My first program clarified the distorted image of the WGBH series with a combination of testimony by veterans and film footage of U.S. troops in combat. Reflections on that theme are encouraged by an accompanying, understated musical theme. The overall effect of the sequence is a feeling of respect for the heroism of American fighting men.

The second program, *Television's Vietnam: The Impact of the Media,* also analyzes the major media coverage of the war, especially widespread misrepresentation of the Tet Offensive in 1968. The battle for Khe Sanh was a lengthy confrontation in the northwest of Vietnam; 6000 Marines defended a base and surrounding hilltops against numerically superior North Vietnamese regular forces. The Marines gained an important victory in a battle still studied at the Marine Corps' Basic School as a classic example of the *successful* static defense. Yet many American news organizations presented Khe Sanh as an American *defeat,* a fact that suggests dishonesty or at least a skewed understanding of the battle, for when the fight was over, the Marines had held their ground against overwhelming numbers of North Vietnamese troops.

Historical accuracy and free speech in filmmaking is hindered by the major networks' policy that denies the use of the taped reports of their correspondents to other media. For example, to comment upon what the major news anchors had said about Khe Sanh—an American victory, not a defeat as commonly portrayed—I was forced to devise my own method of presenting their words and views of the battle. The resulting montage is introduced by General William Westmoreland and stresses the inaccuracy of network reports of the battle. Ironically, in this instance, the networks' policy worked against them.

Education in Critical Viewing

Since the 1930s, the documentary film has been a highly interpretive medium. It is fruitless to deplore it; it is time to take it in hand. Programs such as *Television's Vietnam* should be studied in our schools to teach students how images can be artfully arranged to support a particular viewpoint. Nothing less than our democratic life is endangered when too many Americans believe everything they see on television.

The visually literate student/citizen needs to know how a producer's point of view affects the *entertainment* aspects of television-viewing. In 1964, Stanley Kubrick directed a film, *Dr. Strangelove, or How I Learned to Stop Worrying and Love the Bomb*. The movie, a comic satire, still evokes laughter though it conveys a dangerous message of hopelessness about the prospect of avoiding nuclear war. Students studying such a film should understand satire; they should know that satire thrives on exaggeration and hyperbole. One of the movie's messages, for instance, is that traditional concepts of war no longer apply in the nuclear age; this view is not stated overtly, but through a character named Colonel King Kong. A visually literate student would be able to analyze the historical accuracy—or inaccuracy—of such a movie, and the objectivity—or subjectivity—of Kubrick's story.

In the same vein, one of the most devastating portraits of America's experience in the Vietnam War is Francis Ford Coppola's epic *Apocalypse Now* (1978). Whatever the particular political interpretation presented by Coppola, his film is an ambitious work of imagination. Visually literate students can be taught to appreciate the film's literary roots, because its roots will explain the film's exaggerated depiction of Colonel Kilgore. The characterization ably conveys Coppola's comment on the American military, but its origin is actually in Joseph Conrad's *Heart of Darkness*. This fact explains Colonel Kilgore's inhuman dimensions within the context of the epic story told by both the novel and the film, because Kilgore is Conrad's station master, Kurtz, brought to life on celluloid. The student who is trained to discern the connections between literature and film could differentiate Coppola's dramatic artistic exaggeration of Colonel Kilgore from the elements of mere propaganda.

Anyone interested in fostering a better public understanding of international politics must confront the challenge of the visual media. Currently, American film libraries are full of journalistic productions made by audio-visualists rather than by historians. The examples of distorted history and adversary journalism could be extended *ad infinitum:* in the fall of 1986, for example, PBS aired *The Africans,* a nine-part series that was condemned by historians for compressing the vast complexities of history into a naive Marxist mold.

Factual, interpretive, and methodological errors in filmmaking will persist until historians begin to produce challenging films for classroom study. Only then will our schools be able to teach students to be educated and critical viewers, not passive receptacles for propaganda.

Some Conclusions and Suggestions

THE PRECEDING PAGES present a variety of thoughts and concerns about the teaching of international politics. Most writers agree that schools should prepare young Americans to participate intelligently in the public affairs of the community. There is also general agreement that teachers should avoid propaganda, such as a one-sided or biased presentation of information. This is not easy, of course, because in a free society, controversy swirls around public issues. An inspiring teacher, moreover, is bound to have views, and the mere act of selecting information stresses some facts rather than others, a process that may readily lead to bias.

Certain precautions may minimize these dangers: (1) teachers should be alert to the temptation to propagandize; (2) students should be exposed to teachers with varied points of view; (3) educators should consciously select information necessary to enable students to *understand* the American form of government, its domestic policies, its foreign policies, and international relations.

There are other dangers. The term *politics* underlines the importance of *power* in international relations. The teacher's primary concern in civic education is not with intercultural understanding, or even with tolerance of people of other cultures, but with power relationships; relationships that are inevitable in a world composed of different and competing states. Power is paramount in international politics because complex human groups generate force that may be used in relations with other groups. This force finds expression in attitudes ranging from admiration and friendship to hostility and fear; it brings about alliances, but may also result in war.

Our public schools should reject pressures for special courses on international affairs and the American role in them. Our high schools are already overloaded with special courses that often become instruments of propaganda (or "behavior modification") rather than of education.

International politics for high school consumption should be incorporated into existing social studies curricula: American history, American government, and world history. Teachers would do well to have a checklist of international politics to offer their students. This information may be divided into: the history of American foreign relations and national defense; the major power struggles in world history; political geography; the making and implementing of foreign and defense policies; and the concepts and vocabulary of international relations.

There are obstacles. American history, for example, stands out as the best or most convenient vehicle for teaching about international politics. But as it is, few teachers manage in a single-year course to cover events following World War II. Yet American history up to 1939 has little relevance to the role of the United States as a superpower in the contemporary world.

What can be done? Teachers must first recognize the importance of recent history and their responsibility to teach it. Second, they should insist that a sizeable part of any course in American government deal with foreign and defense policies. In the American history course two methods may help provide adequate coverage of the postwar period: (1) The first few weeks of the course may be devoted to recent history. Although recent events are not "history" in the conventional sense, ignoring them can have disastrous consequences for it contributes to the already severe disadvantage of democratic societies in international politics. (2) Two years of American history could be required in high school—the second year to include a considerable amount of world history as a means of understanding contemporary events.

Courses in American government should devote some time to examining how foreign and defense policies are made. The instruction should also include explanations of important technical terms (see Glossary, Appendix D) and a discussion of various ways of thinking about foreign policy. For example, such terms as: *Realpolitik, legalistic, ideological, Utopian,* and *national interest* suggest various interpretations of historical trends and events. Especially important today is the *Marxist-Leninist* model of international politics because it guides all leaders of the Soviet bloc. Another important contemporary perspective, *moral realism,* attempts to apply the insights of realism and morality to international politics.

World history courses can contribute to understanding international politics and American foreign policy in important ways. More than other required social studies courses, they emphasize geography and geographical relationships.

World history courses should also examine the vulnerability of prosperous, free, civilized societies, their proneness to demoralization, and the consequences they have suffered throughout history—from subjugation to genocide. As Marxism-Leninism correctly teaches, the human condition is marked by fluctuating conflict—a generalization never lost sight of by Communist leaders and hardly ever remembered by complacent democracies. Yet because many history teachers will not acknowledge this general truth, world history courses often ignore the international struggles that have occurred since the rise of civilization. Time and again these struggles have seen less advanced societies overwhelm advanced civilizations, only to rise gradually into a civilized state and be overwhelmed in turn.

Finally, world history courses should deal with the technological and organizational changes that affected the military. These include the use of iron, war-chariots, heavy infantry, the stirrup-firm cavalry, heavily armored cavalry, gunpowder, rifled guns, armored warships, aircraft, tanks, and, in our time, nuclear missiles. The relation of these technical changes to political changes should be noted as well.

Various questions follow from the above. Has the development of nuclear weapons rendered war obsolete? Insofar as minor wars are concerned, the answer is no. As has been mentioned earlier, there have been two hundred conventional wars since World War II. At present, world wars—wars that result in the collapse of a whole civilization—may be impossible. But if this is true today, it may not be true tomorrow. Studies of history cannot be slighted merely because present conditions are unprecedented; human nature has changed little, if any, over the course of human history. It was popular in the 1960s and 1970s to declare that "history is irrelevant"; but, as Bismarck observed, "Fools say that they learn by experience. I prefer to profit by others' experience."

Some teachers worry that teaching about current issues in international politics will expose them to criticism from parents or others who may disagree with a comment or interpretation. But if educators have labored for objectivity, they must be prepared to reply in good conscience that our democratic society cannot allow ignorance or obscurantism to keep knowledge of international politics from our schools.

This does not imply that teachers should avoid comment and explanation. Without embellishment, the sheer facts of history are meaningless and dull. But by stressing the record of events, teachers can guard against selecting material for the purpose of manipulating students, and provide students with the various means—timetables, maps, and glossaries—needed to understand ongoing political events. If, as educators, we could eliminate distracting "short courses" and "electives" and expand the time allotted to required social studies or history courses, we could graduate a much larger number of students equipped to be citizens. We might even hope to break the vicious cyclical process by which one human society after another achieves affluence and freedom only to lose both through a gradual decline into demoralization and defeat.

Introductory Note to the Appendixes

SOME IDEAS FOR teaching international politics and for incorporating the subject in textbooks on history and government in the high school are offered in the following pages. Included are a sample teaching method suited to a high school text, a series of maps, a timeline of international events, and a glossary of international politics. The appendixes are designed to stimulate teachers to engage in creative individual and joint lesson-planning sessions.

I am convinced, from my experience as teacher and program director, that both teachers and students appreciate the challenge of ideas and sophisticated thought, and that both are bored and repelled by simplified approaches to social and political issues. We all become quickly aware of being "talked down" to, and students recognize the difference between forms of history and political analysis that are realistic and true to facts, and those that manipulate or rewrite "the facts" in Orwellian fashion.

Many persons have assisted in preparing this material, but special mention should be made of three volunteers: Patti Wehner, Steve Ryan, and Paula Radcliffe, each of whom gave youthful perspectives and insights as well as research assistance.

Raymond English

APPENDIX A

Examples of Instructional Materials on International Politics for Use in High School

The following sample is based in part on texts and teachers' guides developed under the direction of Raymond English for the Educational Research Council of America. The texts from which material is borrowed are Nations in Action: International Tensions, *and* The American Adventure, *published by Allyn and Bacon, Inc., Boston, Massachusetts, in 1972 and 1977 respectively. (© by the Educational Research Council of America). This incomplete draft outlines teaching approaches that may be used to complement high school texts on American history and government.*

International Politics and Foreign Policy

Politics is competition for power. The competition may be mild and played according to rules, or it may be violent. This is true of international, as well as domestic politics. In domestic politics, the competitors are politicians and parties; in international politics, the competitors are states.

If government forgets that politics is competition for power, it may find that it has lost not only power but freedom as well. In order to keep power and freedom, or *national independence,* statesmen work out a plan of action and defense. This plan is the *foreign policy* of their country.

Since some states are weak and others strong one might expect the weak to be taken over by the strong. Indeed, this has often happened. But two forces work to protect the freedom and independence of small and weak nations. First, the very strong states use their power to prevent the other strong states from becoming too powerful. Second, small nations form *alliances* to protect themselves. They agree to join together to fight a power that attacks any one of them. In this way they set up a *balance of power.*

These ideas may be illustrated from the events following World War II.

1. The weak states of Eastern Europe were taken over by the strong

power of the Soviet Union. These are the Soviet "satellites"—one-party, Communist states. They are linked in an alliance called the *Warsaw Pact*.

2. The states of Western Europe were as weak and exhausted as those of Eastern Europe. They were in danger, but the United States would not allow the Soviet Union to take them over.

3. Then in 1949, the Western European nations, with Canada and the United States, formed an alliance to defend themselves, the *North Atlantic Treaty Organization (NATO)*.

• Look at the map showing the Warsaw Pact and NATO powers. (See Map 3, page 111). Name the Soviet satellites and the states that make up NATO. (Canada and the United States are not shown on this map. Spain joined NATO in 1982.)

• At the end of World War II, the Soviet Union also tried to take over Greece and Turkey, but President Truman promised that the United States would send help to prevent this. This promise was called the *Truman Doctrine*, which was announced in 1947, two years before the North Atlantic Treaty. Which way of keeping small powers independent is illustrated by the Truman Doctrine?

• Are the Truman Doctrine and the North Atlantic Treaty examples of *balance of power* politics? Explain.

Measuring Power

States are not equally powerful. We must recognize, too, that each state's power changes with time. Some grow weaker; some grow stronger.

How can we measure the power of each state? Power, in international politics, seems to depend on a combination of factors:

1. Economic development (industry, capital, technology, wealth, skilled workers, managers, and scientists).

2. Size (land and population).

3. Armed forces (arms and equipment, trained personnel, preparedness, reserves).

4. Spirit of the people (willingness to make sacrifices for defense).

5. Prestige (This is a vague but important factor. Does the nation keep its promises? Is its government tough and persistent? Do its armed forces fight well? Does it support justice and freedom?).

6. Geographical conditions (location, communications, defensibility, foreign bases, dependence on foreign trade).

It is necessary to know a good deal in order to judge the power of a nation. Even then, some things must be weighed that cannot be measured, such as "spirit of the people." (Another term for this is *morale*.) Moreover, these factors vary from time to time. Governments can change from tough to weak, or from intelligent to short-sighted, or the other way round.

Governments actually spend much money and energy trying to get information about the power of other nations. This is called *intelligence;* it includes the use of spies. Governments also spend money to prevent other powers from learning about their secrets and plans; this is *counterintelligence.* Sometimes governments try to deceive their rivals, or to weaken the spirit of a rival people; this is *disinformation,* also called *psychological warfare.*

Finally, power is *relative.* This means that the power of a nation is judged in relation to the power of other nations, especially its potential rivals. It is also judged in relation to its *commitments,* that is, its responsibilities in the world.

• The ideas in this section are diverse but important. See if you can give concrete meaning to various ideas mentioned by dealing with the following problems.

1. Give examples of economically developed and less developed countries.

2. Which nations in the world have the largest land areas? Which have the largest populations?

3. Is the *morale* of the people usually more important in democratic countries such as the United States than it is in dictatorships such as the Soviet Union? Why or why not?

4. The letters KGB and CIA stand for organizations that deal with intelligence as well as counterintelligence. Which countries do they work for?

5. Name some of the *international commitments* of the United States at the present time.

• People often speak of *arms races,* that is, competition among states to keep their armed forces equal to those of rival states. How does the idea that *power is relative* explain "arms races"?

Making Foreign Policy

When statesmen decide on the foreign and defense policies of their country, their first concern is to protect *the national interest* and provide for *national security.*

DECIDING ON FOREIGN POLICY

1. NATIONAL INTEREST AND NATIONAL SECURITY
2. POWER CALCULATIONS
3. GEOGRAPHY AND STRATEGIC CONSIDERATIONS
4. IDEOLOGIES, PRINCIPLES, AND FORMS OF GOVERNMENT
5. HISTORICAL FACTORS

National security means keeping the national interest safe. The country, its people, their property, and economic interests must be protected against attack. This includes safety for citizens outside the country and for trade with foreign lands. If a government fails to provide national security it has failed in its most important duty.

Next in order are calculations of *relative power,* which we examined in the section "Measuring Power." When statemen have made these calculations they can decide how strong their armed forces are or could be, and what alliances they should make to protect their nation against potential enemies. They are also able to decide whether to *compromise or stand firm* in a disagreement with other states.

The calculation of relative power is perhaps the most delicate problem that statesmen face. Knowing the *power equation* is essential in order to make the right *commitments* in international politics.

• Walter Lippmann, a deep thinker about politics, said that a sound foreign policy is one in which *power and commitments are balanced.* Explain what he meant. Do you agree? Give examples of sound and unsound foreign policies.

• Geographic understanding is indispensable. How does the location of our own country affect its interests? What do geographic factors in international politics tell us about *strategy?* Strategy is the overall, long-range plan for achieving an objective.

• Look at a map of the world or a globe. Find Vietnam, Afghanistan, Cuba, and Nicaragua. Note the *spatial relationship* (distance, ease or difficulty of access) between each of these countries and (a) the Soviet Union, and (b) the United States. How would you describe the strategic importance of each small country to each of the large countries?

The political system and the political ideas of a nation will also affect foreign policy. A country such as the United States, with a *constitutional democratic* government, is unlikely to have an *aggressive* and *expansionist* foreign policy. When all citizens vote freely for their government, they seldom choose a government that will start a war of aggression.

Dictatorial governments, however, are not dependent on popular elections. If the few politicians who control domestic power decide to attack another country, they do not need to worry about public opinion or the "next election." Dictatorial governments, moreover, are often linked with *aggressive ideologies.* The Soviet Union, for example, is (or was) committed to the Communist ideology, or *Marxism-Leninism,* which teaches that Communism must conquer the world.

The basic ideas of democracies generally include *equal rights and freedom for all people,* the *rule of law,* and *justice and fairness for all,* together with economic arrangements intended to satisfy *consumers* (private customers). The foreign policy of a democratic nation is therefore often aimed at defending or expanding human rights and democratic institutions. President Eisenhower's book about his work as supreme commander of Allied Forces in Europe in World War II was called *Crusade in Europe*. He thought of the war as a "crusade" for freedom and democracy. Foreign policy is not mainly concerned with wars, however. It includes many unwarlike activities. A strong nation can protect human rights by *diplomatic pressure* on other countries.

Finally, persons making foreign policy must also know history: the history of their own country and of the countries they are dealing with. Economic conditions in all countries with which the policy is concerned must be considered also.

In most cases, the recent history of international relations is the essential clue to immediate foreign policy issues. The history of the United States in the nineteenth century would not tell us much about the power and the problems of the United States since 1945.

On the other hand, the events of the nineteenth century are far from unimportant. The Monroe Doctrine tells much about America's strategic interests. And Latin American countries have not forgotten the annexation of Texas and the Mexican War.

• In December 1904, President Theodore Roosevelt announced what became known as the "Roosevelt Corollary to the Monroe Doctrine." This corollary stated that the United States would, if necessary, exercise "international police power" to ensure that Latin American states made good their obligations to foreign countries. A year before, the United States had encouraged Panama to secede from Colombia so that Americans could build the Panama Canal. Why have these historical facts been held against the United States by Latin Americans?

There are other considerations in making foreign policy. Trade routes may be vital in some cases. Military bases may change the balance of power in some parts of the world. Changes in technology may effect economic strength or military defense. Some persons argue that nuclear weapons have made all traditional ideas about international politics irrelevant. Others say that the old rules about deterring aggression by strong armed forces still apply, but that a new danger is that some great invention, or breakthrough, in military technology might give one nation such superior power that the rest of the world would be at its mercy.

These special cases will be examined later.

United States Foreign Policy Since World War II: Relations with the Soviet Union

In the second half of the twentieth century, two states possess so much power that either of them can defy all the remaining states. These two states—the Soviet Union and the United States—are called *superpowers,* to distinguish them from the "great powers" of the past.

In addition to the elements of power listed in the box on page 97, the superpowers have overwhelming supplies of nuclear weapons. It is often asserted that each has sufficient nuclear arms to destroy most of the human race. The two superpowers have competed with each other not only in the number of nuclear weapons, but also in technology and scientific research.

Why are the two superpowers rivals for influence and control in the world and even in outer space? Probably rivalry is inevitable between two nearly equal and very powerful states.

• Look at a globe or map of the world. Compare the location and size of the superpowers. Why are these two states so much more powerful than other countries in an age of missiles and long-distance bombers?

• In 1835 the French writer, Alexis de Tocqueville, published the first part of *Democracy in America.* The following excerpts are from its final pages:

> There are now two great nations in the world which, starting from different points, seem to be advancing toward the same goal: the Russians and the Anglo-Americans.
> Both have grown in obscurity, while the world's attention was occupied elsewhere, they have suddenly taken their place among the leading nations, making the world take note of their birth and of their greatness almost at the same instant.
>
> *   *   *
>
> The American fights against natural obstacles; the Russian is at grips with men. The former combats the wilderness and barbarism; the latter, civilization with all its arms. America's conquests are made with the plowshare, Russia's with the sword.
> To attain their aims, the former relies on personal interest and gives free scope to the unguided strength and common sense of individuals.
> The latter in a sense concentrates the whole power of society in one man.
> One has freedom as the principal means of action; the other has servitude.
> Their point of departure is different and their paths diverse; nevertheless, each seems called by some secret design of Providence one day to hold in its hands the destinies of half the world.

Why could Tocqueville make so striking a prediction? What contrast does he see in the social *values* of Americans and Russians?

The rivalry between the United States and the Soviet Union (formerly the Russian Empire) seems to be unusually severe because of moral contrasts between them. The United States is leader of the *Free World,* that is, of nations with market economies where private persons own most business enterprises, and in which there are free elections, free speech, and a free press. The Soviet Union is leader of the *Communist* nations, where the state owns the factories in a *command economy* and controls all publication, broadcasting, and education, and where there is only one political party—the Communist Party.

These differences between the political and economic systems of the superpowers make the competition for power very intense. At the root of the differences is *ideological conflict,* which is comparable to the religious conflicts that divided the world during the Crusades, or during the Wars of Religion that followed the Reformation.

The Soviet Union is tied to the ideology of *Marxism-Leninism,* which teaches that conflict between "capitalist" societies and "socialist" societies is inevitable, and that the socialist, or Communist, societies must conquer the whole world. The ideology of Marxism-Leninism is *totalitarian,* that is, it exerts total control and it calls for total obedience and total loyalty on the part of everyone living under it.

The United States and the Free World do not have an "ideology" in this totalitarian sense. Their central idea is *freedom,* which cannot coexist with the belief that only one political party or only one view of human life is absolutely correct. The Free World consists of "open" societies, where there is free trade in ideas as well as in goods.

- Why is freedom incompatible with totalitarianism?
- Give some examples of contrasts between the lives of people in the totalitarian Soviet Union and the democratic United States.
- Why is a democratic society an "open society" and a totalitarian society "closed"?

Theories of International Politics

Groups produce tensions owing to misunderstandings of one another as well as to real conflicts of interest and values. We are, for better or worse, members of our nation and culture groups. We share certain values and certain interests. We have no alternative—if our values and interests are to be protected—to being loyal to our group. As normal human beings we can hardly switch our values, interests, and perspectives to those of a Peking Communist or a member of the *Volkspolizei* in East Berlin. The best we can do is to try to understand something of their attitudes without sacrificing our loyalty to our own group.

A number of options are open to us as we attempt to analyze international relations and make prudent judgments about them. Some are more helpful than others, and sometimes a combination of approaches is necessary.

Perhaps the least useful approach is the Utopian approach. The user of this method sets up some standard of perfection, and then proceeds to judge actual political affairs against it. Perfect peace, world government, total disarmament, pacifism, abolition of all prejudice and economic inequality—these are some examples of Utopian standards or objectives. They may indicate goodness of heart, but not strength of mind or depth of knowledge.

Another approach is the *legalistic-moralistic* approach, which is similar to utopianism, but a little more realistic. The legalistic-moralistic theorist sets up certain norms of international behavior—rigid international laws—and tries to judge cases of tension and conflict as if brought before a court of law. He asks such questions as, who is the aggressor? How shall he be punished? Can the punishment deter others? Can we declare the case closed? The trouble is that international tensions are seldom capable of being resolved into neat categories of bad states versus good states, or lawbreakers versus law-abiders. There is, moreover, no impartial court to try the case. And even if such existed, its ruling would have to be enforced by armies

The following pages are excerpted (with some modifications) from the Teacher's Guide to *Nations in Action: International Tensions,* by the Social Science Staff of the Educational Research Council of America, Boston, Allyn and Bacon, 1972.—*Ed.*

raised by states that very probably would have axes of their own to grind.

The legalistic-moralistic approach has its uses in many minor instances, but cannot settle the more serious cases where conflicts of values, interests, and power occur. The most important international tensions are political, not legal; that is to say, they result from clashes of power and will in a world of shifting forces.

So we are driven to other theoretical approaches. Not far removed from legalism-moralism is the *ideological,* or crusading approach. This takes many forms. A common factor, however, seems to be the assumption that one side (one's own) is good, and the other side, necessarily, is evil. International conflicts or tensions are assumed to be battles between right and wrong. Thus, for example, Soviet leaders speak of the United States and its allies as "capitalist warmongers." They predict the defeat of this evil force by their own self-styled peace-loving ideology that they say represents the interest of the working class the world over.

Adherents of the anti-Communist ideology denounce "Godless, atheistic Communism," "Communist aggression," and "totalitarian slave systems" as the enemy that must sooner or later be destroyed by the "free world."

The ideological approach is undoubtedly effective. During a major war, the temptation to use ideological propaganda is almost irresistible. Thus, in World War II, the Allies grandly described themselves as defenders of justice, freedom, and democracy, and denounced their enemies as militaristic aggressors and criminals. Clearly, on such terms, the war could only end with the total defeat, unconditional surrender, and punishment of the wicked offenders. Whether such tactics were really helpful in the end is doubtful.

In other circumstances, ideological approaches may place serious obstacles in the way of rational foreign policy decisions. They may lead to head-on confrontation and global war, even though the basic *interests* of both sides (as opposed to their ideological commitments) are harmed rather than helped by such a confrontation. In any case, ideology seems an uncertain tool. The Soviet Union and Yugoslavia were committed to Marxism-Leninism in 1945; by 1948 they had broken off relations. Similarly, the Soviet Union and the People's Republic of China, both claiming to represent the pure Communist ideology, became bitterly hostile by 1960. On the other side, common ideological assumptions have failed to keep France's armed forces under unified NATO command and have not prevented friendly relations between the United States and left-wing regimes like that of Marshal Tito and the People's Republic of China.

Marxism-Leninism is not only an ideology. It is also a theory of international politics that claims to be "scientific." As a theory, Marxism-Leninism begins with the assumption that conflict is inevitable and unceasing in human affairs. There is no such thing as "peace"; there is only a variable intensity of conflict, ranging from open war to subdued competition and maneuvering for advantage. The latter condition is what the Soviet leader Khrushchev called "peaceful coexistance"—a condition that, he said, would end with the "burial" of the United States and capitalism. Mao Zedong summed up the Marxist-Leninist theory as "protracted conflict."

According to the theory, conflict will persist until the final conquest of this whole human race by the Communist powers. At that point a radical change in human nature will begin, and when the change is complete human beings will be as docile and peaceful as bees in a hive.

One need not pay serious attention to the ultimate Utopian vision. It is unlikely that any adherent of Marxism-Leninism treats it as a possibility. However, the theory of protracted and inevitable conflict should be borne in mind; it is an indispensable key to understanding Soviet and Soviet-bloc foreign and defense policy.

Other approaches are variations of the theory based on the idea of *national interest;* the assumption that every political group has certain basic interests. The group must maintain itself as a group—protect its own members, maintain their way of life, defend its territory, and so on. To some persons, this approach seems unprincipled, lacking in idealism and generous commitment to justice.

In its extreme form, the theory of national interest can be most unprincipled. Machiavelli, for example, carried the idea to the point of justifying any action that would increase one's power. He argued that a state could make agreements and treaties with the sole purpose of breaking them when the potential enemy was off his guard.

The national interest approach need not—indeed it should not—involve such unscrupulous amorality. Extreme Machiavellian policies are self-defeating, for the interest of any nation includes its being respected by other nations, that is, having a reputation for honor.

The theory of national interest can be the foundation of various types of policy. It may lead to *imperialism,* that is, expansion and conquest, either for the sake of more power and economic advantage, or to provide buffer zones, or to counterbalance other imperialistic powers. Most nations, however, are mainly concerned with maintaining their independence and preserving their national interests. Hence the *balance of power* policy, which is designed to check imperialistic aggression by stronger powers against weaker ones. The balance of power operates by producing a sufficient concentration of military power to deter a would-be aggressor from gambling on a quick and profitable victory. Weaker states may join in alliances guaranteeing collective action in the event of attack on any one of them; they may also engage in armament policies designed to make the cost of aggression outweigh the expected gains.

Authoritarian or totalitarian states are generally far more capable of engaging in long-term preparations for aggression than are popularly governed states. For one thing, taxes and appropriations for armaments cannot be challenged outside the small governing clique. For another, public opinion can be manipulated by the government's control of the mass media. Finally, censorship, secret police, and the like can be highly efficient in totalitarian states in preventing the leakage of information about weapons or military plans. For these reasons the balance of power is a vitally important policy for democratic states.

Even better than the balance of power might be a system of *worldwide collective security,* that is, a system in which all states would automatically come to the aid of any nation under attack. This vision gave birth to both the League of Nations and the United Nations organizations. Unfortunately, worldwide collective security is very difficult to achieve; it is a legalistic-moralistic vision, based on the assumption that all nations will recognize the same international laws and will interpret them impartially and unanimously. That situation is not yet in existence: nations line up in blocs according to their particular national interest; they do not agree on the identity of the aggressor. Some are totalitarian. Some are very powerful. Some are very weak. Few nations are prepared to sacrifice men and money to ensure justice on the other side of the world.

Thus, apart from the superpowers, most states tend to rely on maintaining the balance of power by *regional security* arrangements, such as the North Atlantic Treaty Organization and its counterpart, the Warsaw Pact. Sometimes, even regional security arrangements are inadequate. The Middle East, Africa, Southeast Asia, and the Indian subcontinent are insecure and unstable, and apparently incapable of setting up local organizations for collective security. In such areas, the influence of the superpowers, with their global concerns of mutual counterbalance, tends to be strong and not always conducive to stability.

An additional theory to be taken into account is *mutual deterrence.* This theory takes various forms. In its most obvious form it is simply a version of the balance of power: rival states or blocs maintain sufficient armaments in a state of readiness to make a sudden attack by the other side too risky and costly to be worth gambling on. In the 1960s and 1970s nuclear deterrence took the form of *Mutual Assured Destruction* (MAD), according to which, each of the superpowers maintained a large stock of intercontinental missiles, targeted on its rival's population centers, so that if either superpower started a nuclear exchange, *both* nations would be destroyed.

This system of "counter-value targeting" gave place in the late 1970s and the 1980s to "counter-force targeting," that is, to aiming the nuclear ICBMs at the rival power's ICBMs, with a view to destroying them before flight and so making retaliation impossible or inadequate. This policy gave rise to fears of "pre-emptive first strike," a surprise attack that would place the rival power at the mercy of the attacker.

The system of mutual deterrence when nuclear missiles are the main deterrent, requires rival powers to be continuously alert both with intelligence services and devices to give early warning of attack and with scientific and technological research designed to forestall a breakthrough that might give the rival power a decisive advantage.

Although the principle of mutual nuclear deterrence is vitally important in preventing a major devastating world war, we should note that this massive deterrence will not prevent many relatively minor conventional wars, nor will it prevent the erosion of the prestige and influence of a great power. Nuclear deterrence cannot be used as a sanction against the aggressions, imperial expansions, wars of liberation, guerrilla warfare, and terrorist subversion of which we have seen so many examples since 1950, especially in the Third World.

The last theory to be dealt with is associated with the term *geopolitics*. Geopolitical theories are based on two assumptions: that man is a creature governed by the "territorial imperative," that is, the need to possess and control land in order to ensure his survival; and that since the physical features of the earth are more or less fixed for long periods of time, they dictate to a considerable degree the political behavior of states.

As in the case of national interest theory, the geopolitical theory has many possible proliferations. A simple example is the idea that there are *natural frontiers*. French foreign policy for hundreds of years was directed to expand and establish France's natural (easily defensible) frontiers—the Rhine, the Alps, the Pyrenees.

Another aspect of geopolitical theory is concerned with the implication of the *relative locations* of political units. Nations or states that share common frontiers are liable to squabble over their borders or compete for influence among their neighbors. Some geopoliticians predicted correctly that the Soviet Union and Communist China would come into opposition over control of central Asia.

Location also helps to explain the lines on which foreign policy, especially expansion, will develop. Thus England (later Great Britain) was led to policies of overseas expansion and trade through its location on the Atlantic.

Another geographic factor in international relations is the location of *barriers* and their opposites—*lines of communication*. For thousands of years certain major obstacles to communication (and direct conflict) existed: great mountain ranges such as the Himalayas, deserts like the Gobi, ice caps, rain forests, and oceans. Technology has in the course of time changed some of this—from the advances in shipbuilding in the fifteenth century to present-day aircraft and intercontinental ballistic missiles, which have at least modified the effectiveness of many great natural barriers.

Finally, one must mention the great geopolitical *Mackinder-Spykman Theory* which is based on the arrangements of the world's landmasses. It offers a useful and plausible explanation of Soviet-American relations since 1945. The British geographer, Sir Halford Mackinder wrote long ago:

> Who rules East Europe commands the Heartland [largely Russia, Siberia, and northern China]. Who rules the Heartland commands the World-Island [Eurasia and Africa]. Who rules the World-Island commands the World.

"Command" in these sentences implies, "will ultimately dominate and conquer."

Years later, the American geographer Nicholas Spykman argued that Mackinder's thesis left out an important factor, the "Rimland", that is, the peripheral areas of the Eurasian continent (Western Europe, the Mediterranean and Middle East, India, Southeast Asia, Southern China, and Japan). Thus Spykman, looking at the World-Island from the oceans rather than from the Heartland, postulated:

> Who controls the Rimland rules Eurasia; who rules Eurasia controls the destinies of the world.

Notice that the Soviet Union since World War II has worked on the Mackinder hypothesis, using its Heartland control to project its power into the Rimland and beyond. Meanwhile the United States and NATO allies have effectively held on to the European Rimland; the United States has also cultivated the friendship of China, defended South Korea, brought Japan into its orbit, striven to maintain influence in the Middle East, and fought (not entirely successfully) to protect Southeast Asia from Heartland expansion.

APPENDIX C

Maps

The following indicates the type of maps that should be used in textbooks or other instructional materials to illustrate U.S. foreign policy and ensure that students understand location and spatial relations. Additional maps are needed to show the Middle East, Africa, the South Pacific, Afghanistan, and the Northwest frontier of Pakistan and India. It would be useful to have other maps of polar air routes, great circle routes, and the "chokepoints" on sea lanes (Straits of Hormuz, Malacca, Suez, Gibraltar, Cape of Good Hope, the Caribbean, and Panama).

Map 1. Geopolitical Theories of Mackinder and Spykman

This is explained in Appendix B, ''Theories of International Politics.''
It should be compared with the maps showing Soviet expansion.

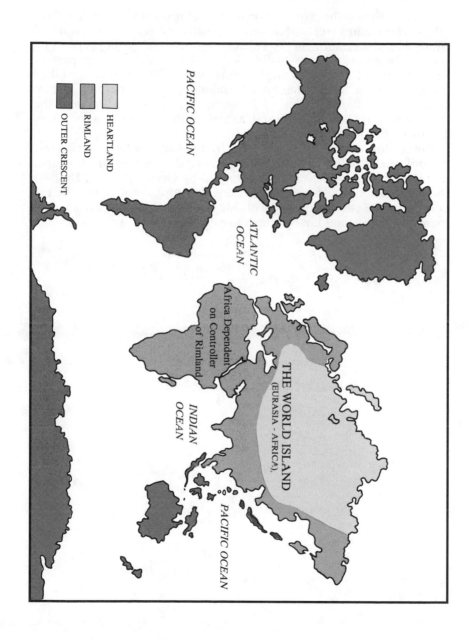

Map 2. Soviet Expansion to 1940

This map shows the Soviet expansion before World War II (1917–1940). The victims were: Mongolia (currently the People's Republic of Mongolia), the eastern part of Poland (as a result of the nonaggression pact between Hitler and Stalin, August 1939), the eastern part of Finland (Soviet forces attacked Finland in late 1939 and were stalled by the Finnish army; the Soviet Union had to settle for part of Finland), the Baltic States of Estonia, Latvia, and Lithuania, the eastern part of Ukraine, Bessarabia, and northern Bukovina (northern Bukovina had been part of Romania).

During the course of World War II, the Soviets temporarily lost control of the Baltic States, Poland, Bessarabia, Bukovina, Ukraine, and Byelorussia, which were all occupied by German forces. By 1945 the Soviets not only recovered all these territories, but converted the countries of Eastern Europe—Poland, Czechoslovakia, Hungary, Romania, Bulgaria, and East Germany—into dependent satellites.

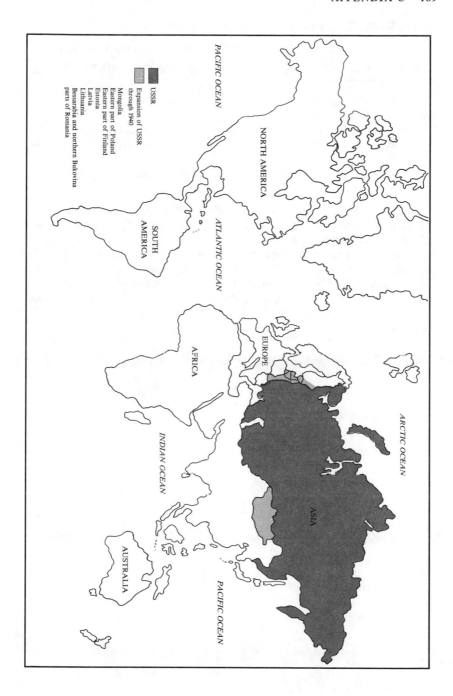

Map 3. Soviet Expansion in Europe, 1935–1945

This shows in detail the situation in Europe after World War II.

1. Finland was rendered helplessly neutral. (See GLOSSARY "Finlandization").
2. The Soviets regained the Baltic States, Bessarabia, Bukovina, and part of Poland.
3. A *cordon sanitaire*—"safety zone"—of satellite Communist states was established in Eastern Europe (contrary to the Yalta and Potsdam Agreements).
4. Yugoslavia and Albania became Communist but did not become satellites.

The "Iron Curtain," dubbed as such by Winston Churchill in March 1946, ran from Stettin in the Baltic to Trieste on the Adriatic: later it moved east of Yugoslavia and Albania.

Austria was under joint occupation of Soviet, American, French, and British forces until 1955, when it regained independence and declared itself, like Sweden and Switzerland, "permanently neutral."

Note that NATO was established to check further Soviet expansion in Europe; the Rimland in Europe is still outside the power of the Heartland State.

ICELAND

ATLANTIC OCEAN

NORWAY

SWEDEN

FINLAND

BALTIC
SEA

IRELAND

NORTH
SEA

DENMARK

SOVIET UNION

UNITED
KINGDOM

NETHERLANDS

EAST
GERMANY

BERLIN

POLAND

BELGIUM

WEST
GERMANY

CZECHOSLOVAKIA

FRANCE

SWITZ.

AUSTRIA

HUNGARY

ROMANIA

PORTUGAL

YUGOSLAVIA

SPAIN

ITALY

BULGARIA

ALBANIA

GREECE

TURKEY

Warsaw Pact 1955

European Members NATO
1952

MEDITERRANEAN SEA

0   100 200 300 400 500 600

miles

AFRICA

Map 4. The Korean War

The following maps separate the Korean War into four stages. The first shows the successful North Korean attack, June–September 1950. The North Koreans forced the U.N. forces into the small area around Pusan, South Korea, and General MacArthur was gathering U.N. troops on the islands of Japan for a major counterattack.

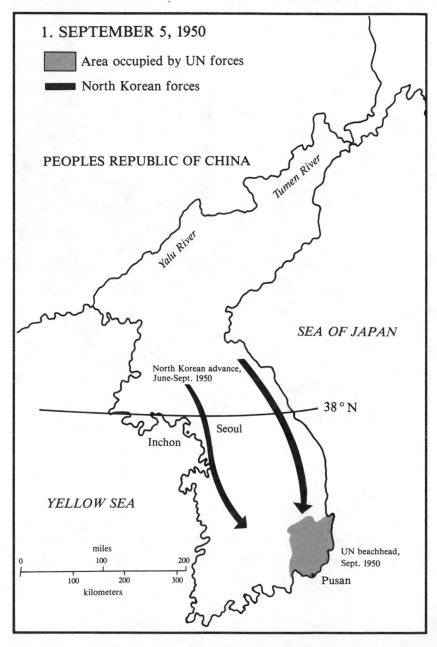

1. SEPTEMBER 5, 1950

Area occupied by UN forces

North Korean forces

PEOPLES REPUBLIC OF CHINA

Tumen River

Yalu River

SEA OF JAPAN

North Korean advance, June–Sept. 1950

38°N

Seoul

Inchon

YELLOW SEA

miles

0   100   200

100   200   300

kilometers

UN beachhead, Sept. 1950

Pusan

The second situation shows the successful counterattack that was launched by the United Nations. Instead of landing at the Pusan beachhead, which the North Koreans had expected, the U.N. force landed in Inchon, cutting off the supply lines of the North Koreans and forcing their retreat in disorder. After this victory the U.N. forces pushed into North Korea, far beyond the 38th parallel. This counterattack started in September and was halted in November of 1950.

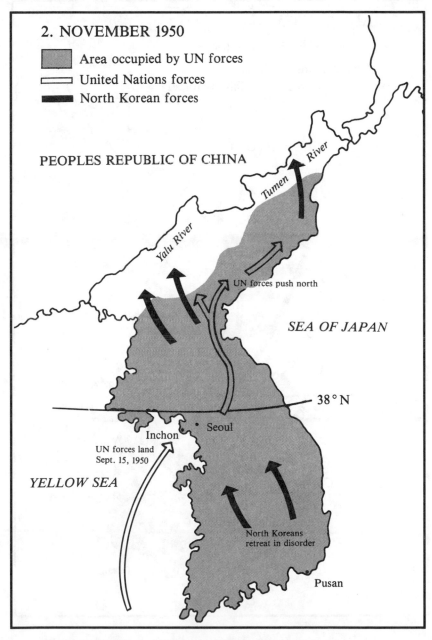

2. NOVEMBER 1950

▨ Area occupied by UN forces
▭ United Nations forces
▬ North Korean forces

PEOPLES REPUBLIC OF CHINA

Tumen River

Yalu River

UN forces push north

SEA OF JAPAN

38° N

Inchon   • Seoul

UN forces land
Sept. 15, 1950

YELLOW SEA

North Koreans
retreat in disorder

Pusan

This halt marked the start of the third stage of the Korean War. The U.N. forces had penetrated so far into North Vietnam that Communist China entered the Korean War on the side of the North Koreans. With the aid of the Chinese army the North Koreans soon pushed the U.N. troops, who had overextended their supply lines, back to the 38th parallel.

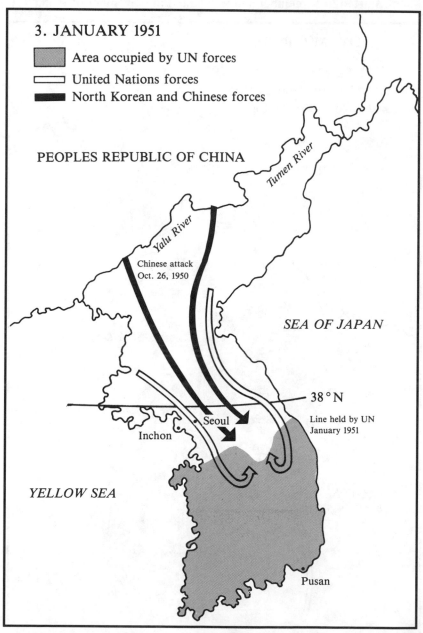

3. JANUARY 1951

▨ Area occupied by UN forces
▭ United Nations forces
▬ North Korean and Chinese forces

PEOPLES REPUBLIC OF CHINA

Tumen River

Yalu River

Chinese attack
Oct. 26, 1950

SEA OF JAPAN

38° N

Seoul

Line held by UN
January 1951

Inchon

YELLOW SEA

Pusan

The fourth and final stage of the Korean War, which lasted from January 1951 to July 1953, was a stalemate a few kilometers north of the former boundary between North and South Korea. When the war finally came to a close this became the demilitarized zone between the two Koreas.

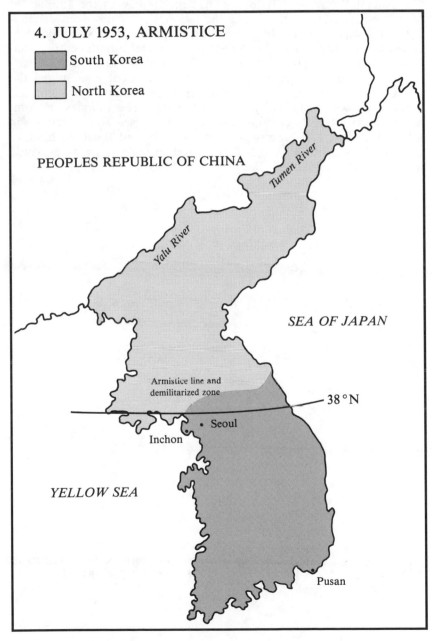

4. JULY 1953, ARMISTICE

South Korea

North Korea

PEOPLES REPUBLIC OF CHINA

Tumen River

Yalu River

SEA OF JAPAN

Armistice line and demilitarized zone

38°N

Seoul

Inchon

YELLOW SEA

Pusan

Map 5. The Communist Threat in Southeast Asia

President Johnson used this map in his autobiography, *The Vantage Point*, to show how he viewed the Communist threat to Southeast Asia in 1965.

President Sukarno of Indonesia had planned, with the support of Mao Tse-tung (Zedong), to make the Indonesian government dependent on the support of the Indonesian Communist Party. Since Mao had called the United States "a paper tiger" several months earlier, Sukarno was ready to align himself with the People's Republic of China.

The U.S. intervention in the Vietnamese conflict encouraged the anti-Communist forces in Indonesia to revolt against President Sukarno, who was replaced by General Suharto. The Indonesian Communist Party—largely composed of ethnic Chinese—was wiped out in a brutal massacre. It seems probable that without the U.S. military presence in Southeast Asia, Indonesia and possibly other states would have become Communist. (See Glossary, "Domino Theory.")

From *The Vantage Point: Perspectives of the Presidency 1963–69* by Lyndon Baines Johnson. Copyright © 1971 by HEC Public Affairs Foundation. Reprinted by permission of Henry Holt & Company, Inc.

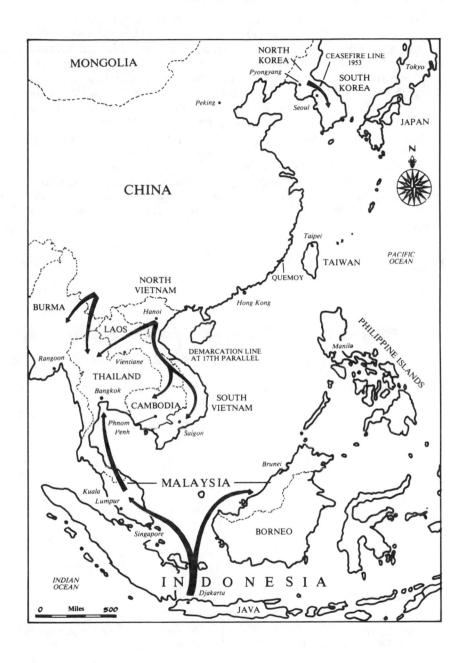

Map 6. Strategic Dilemma in Southeast Asia

President Johnson used this map to show how North Vietnam infiltrated weapons and troops into South Vietnam by land and sea. Most of the sea infiltration had been blocked by 1966, although supplies continued to pass through Sihanoukville in southwest Cambodia. The land infiltration was mainly by the Ho Chi Minh Trail, which extended through Laos and Cambodia. Congress was opposed to escalating the war by bombing the countries through which the trail ran; this increased the difficulty of blocking supplies from North Korea.

The map and the situation it illustrates help to explain the frustration of American strategists in the Vietnam War. The war was to be "limited," and the memory of the debacle in Korea, when the Chinese intervened, haunted American military leaders, who were afraid of a similar blow if they invaded Laos and Cambodia to strangle the supply lines or if they invaded North Vietnam to defeat the Communists at the source.

From *The Vantage Point: Perspectives of the Presidency 1963–69* by Lyndon Baines Johnson. Copyright © 1971 by HEC Public Affairs Foundation. Reprinted by permission of Henry Holt & Company, Inc.

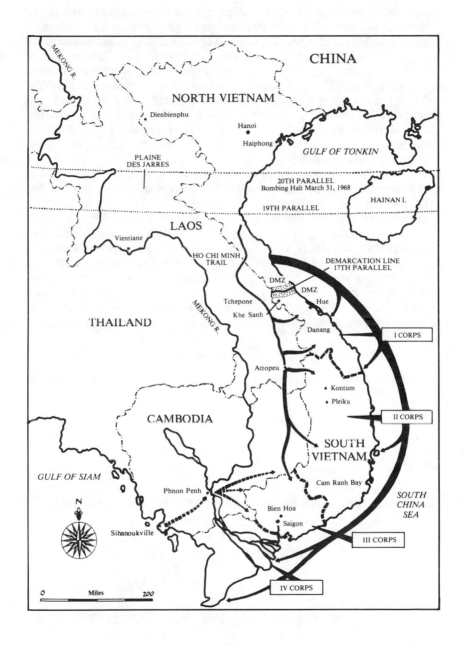

Map 7. Central America and the Caribbean

This shows Soviet expansion and attempted expansion in the United States' "backyard." It indicates the strategic significance of Central America and the Caribbean. A large proportion of U.S. seaborne trade transits the Gulf of Mexico and the Caribbean. The Panama Canal remains an important naval and mercantile link between the Atlantic and Pacific (though not as vital as it was before air transport). Cuba is only 100 miles from Florida; Nicaragua is well placed to attack and destabilize all the small countries of Central America; and the region shown can supply large numbers of Spanish-speaking and English-speaking mercenaries for use in Latin America and Africa, as Cuban mercenaries are already used.

Note the strategic location of Grenada, where a big airstrip was under construction by Cuban and other Communist personnel at the time of the American liberation of the island.

Just before 1980 the Jamaican government headed by Michael Manley was negotiating a close tie with Cuba. The success of Edward Seaga in the election of 1980 probably saved the island nation from becoming a satellite of Cuba and the USSR. The Reagan administration attempted not very successfully to encourage economic revival and development in the Caribbean by means of the "Caribbean Basin Initiative." The region remains a serious problem for American security.

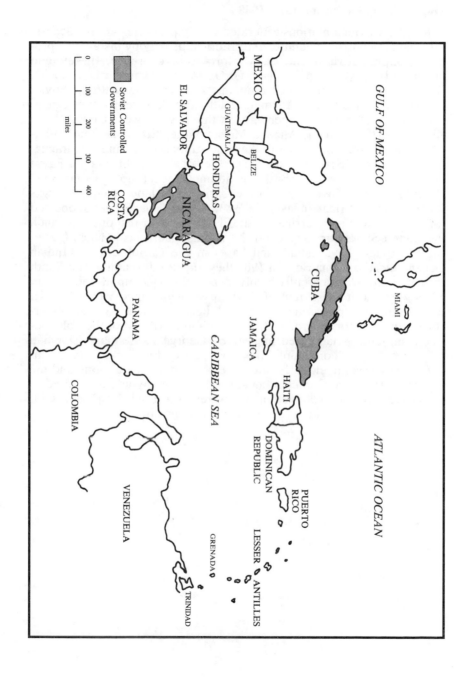

Map 8. Soviet Expansion 1970–1988

After 1945 Soviet ambitions generated steady pressure—often success-ful—to gain control of additional territories, usually by installing a pro-Soviet puppet government. Early efforts to take Greece, Turkey, and northern Iran were blocked (see GLOSSARY: "Truman Doctrine"). Dependencies that remained Communist but broke ties with the Soviet Union were: Yugoslavia, Albania, and the People's Republic of China. Countries that became dependent on the Soviets were Cuba, North Korea, North Vietnam, Angola, Mozambique, Ethiopia, South Viet-nam, Laos, Cambodia, South Yemen, Afghanistan, and Nicaragua. Libya, Iraq, and Syria became close allies of the Soviets (as did Egypt for a time) In the Caribbean an attempt to set up a Communist government and Soviet base in the Caribbean island of Grenada was foiled by an American invasion in 1983. In the 1980s, Soviet-supported forces were waging guerrilla war in El Salvador, in response to which the United States supported anti-Communist guerrillas in Nicaragua.

The Soviets have established bases in the Caribbean, the Indian Ocean, and the China Sea. In 1987 they appeared to aim at the South Pacific, and were apparently involved in a military coup in Fiji.

As we look at the extent of Soviet expansion since World War II, the meaning of "peaceful coexistence" becomes clear. We can under-stand, too, the cogency of Walter Lippmann's critique of the policy of "containment," elaborated in 1947 by George F. Kennan. Lippman pointed out that "containing" the Soviet Union by blocking its expan-sive moves was hopeless, because the perimeter was too long and the places where expansion could occur were too many and too varied to be blocked by American action. We were confronted, Lippmann said, by a "Cold War," which we must learn to wage effectively.

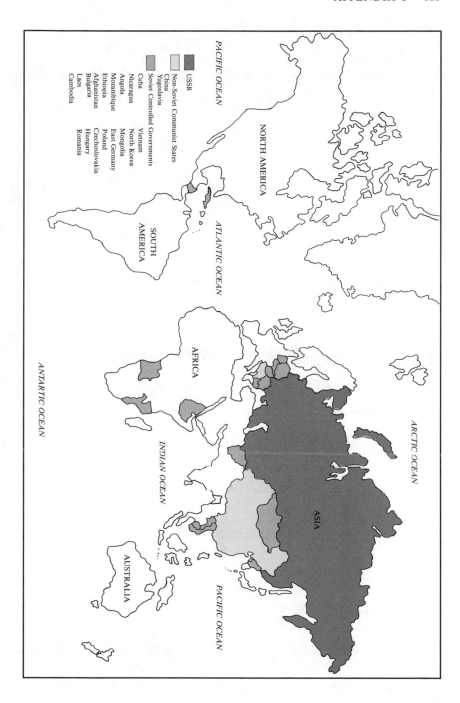

International Politics—Glossary

Aggression—An unjustified attack on one state by another (the AGGRESSOR). In theory, AGGRESSORS are to be condemned and punished by the UNITED NATIONS; in practice, international law and U.N. condemnations are strongly influenced by politics. See COLLECTIVE SECURITY.

Alliance—An agreement/treaty between or among states, usually for common defense and security. Members of an alliance are ALLIES.

Antiballistic Missile (ABM)—A missile designed to intercept intercontinental ballistic missiles (ICBMS). Limited by the ABM Treaty (1972).

Arbitration—Settling a dispute between two powers by referring it to a third party for judgment. Argentina and Chile, for example, referred their dispute over the Beagle Channel and certain islands to the Pope.

Arms Control—Agreements between states to limit or reduce armaments. These may involve extremely complicated terms and systems of inspection or VERIFICATION.

Arms Race—Competition between states in which one side tries to gain the advantage in arms over the other.

Balance of Payments—The debts and credits between trading nations. BALANCE OF TRADE is that part of the BALANCE OF PAYMENTS that is in goods (imported and exported).

Balance of Power—Policy by which states form shifting alliances to prevent any one state or group of states from becoming too powerful. Some hold that BALANCE OF POWER is the basic scientific "law" of international politics. In other words, conflicts will occur when power is unbalanced, and the end of conflict brings some kind of restored equilibrium of power. Without such a "law," the world would presumably fall under the rule of one state.

Balance of Terror—The situation of the superpowers and their allies during a period when nuclear war would bring devastation to both countries. See MUTUAL ASSURED DESTRUCTION.

Blockade—Military action to prevent goods or persons from entering or leaving a country.

Brezhnev Doctrine—Policy enunciated by Soviet leader Leonid Brezhnev in November 1968 to justify Soviet and Warsaw Pact armed intervention to suppress revolt in Czechoslovakia. He asserted the right of SOCIALIST (i.e., COMMUNIST) powers to intervene whenever attempts are made to overthrow any Communist government. In other words, once a country has been taken over by Communists, it cannot change to another form of government.

Central Intelligence Agency (CIA)—The U.S. foreign intelligence organization responsible for gathering information on foreign powers.

Cold War—See under WAR.

Collective Security—Concerted action by all nations to preserve international peace: the theory underlying the League of Nations and the United Nations. More limited examples of collective security are found in regional defense pacts such as NATO, the OAS, and the now defunct SEATO (Southeast Asia Treaty Organization). Global collective security has so far been a failure, because the political interests and values of the nations concerned are so varied that they cannot agree on identifying and punishing "the aggressor."

Command Economy, or Planned Economy—National economy in which production and distribution priorities are set by the central government. Its extreme form is a TOTALITARIAN ECONOMY, as in the Soviet Union. The opposite is a MARKET ECONOMY. Most free-world economies today are MIXED ECONOMIES, in which there are elements of private and state enterprise, of free market and state controls. See also PERESTROIKA.

Comparative Advantage, or Comparative Cost—The principle on which trade among different geographic areas, including nation-states, is based. The well-being and wealth of all areas will be maximized if each specializes in producing the goods it can produce most efficiently. Generally the advantage of certain areas or societies over others is not absolute, but comparative; hence the term.

Constitutionalism—Characteristic of governments whose power and authority are limited by law and convention, that is, by a CONSTITU-

TION, whether written or unwritten. Hence the contrast between CONSTITUTIONAL DEMOCRACY and TOTALITARIAN DEMOCRACY, or CONSTITUTIONAL MONARCHY and ABSOLUTE MONARCHY.

Containment—U.S. policy toward the USSR after the COLD WAR began in 1947 (see WAR). It sought to prevent any further expansion of Soviet control, but proved impossible to carry out effectively. Cf. TRUMAN DOCTRINE, EISENHOWER DOCTRINE. The KOREAN WAR (1950–53) and VIETNAM WAR (1964–75) were applications of CONTAINMENT policy. See REAGAN DOCTRINE.

Cuban Missile Crisis—In October 1962, President John F. Kennedy announced that America had photographs of missile bases being built by the Soviets in Cuba, endangering American cities. The president demanded dismantling of the bases and announced a naval blockade to prevent delivery of missiles to Cuba. Soviet Premier Nikita Khrushchev announced the withdrawal and abandonment of the bases, when the United States promised never to attack Cuba. The crisis ended in November, and the United States has had to tolerate a pro-Soviet dictatorship in Cuba ever since. One effect of the Cuban Missile Crisis has been that Soviet and U.S. leaders have avoided any further *direct confrontation* between their countries' armed forces.

De Facto (Latin: "in fact")—Existing in fact; describes governments or situations that are not legitimate—DE JURE (Latin: "according to law")—but must be accepted at least for a time.

Détente—Reduction of tension between states and so a lessening of chance of war. The term was much used in the 1970s to describe the relaxation of the COLD WAR and arms race between America and the Soviet Union.

Deterrence—A combination of policies and weapons designed to inhibit hostile actions by making such actions too risky and too costly. See BALANCE OF TERROR and MUTUAL ASSURED DESTRUCTION (MAD).

Diplomacy—The conduct of foreign policy and international relations, carried out by DIPLOMATS, such as officials in foreign ministries (U.S. State Department), and ambassadors and embassy staffs. DIPLOMATIC IMMUNITY protects diplomats from coercion and harassment on foreign soil.

Disinformation—Technique of deception used by governments to spread false information. It is used principally by the USSR, which takes advantage of the freedom and openness of Western democracies. See NEWSPEAK.

Economic Growth—Process of increasing productive power in a nation's economy, and thus increasing national income. Countries can be divided into ADVANCED (or DEVELOPED), DEVELOPING, and UNDER-DEVELOPED (or LESS DEVELOPED) COUNTRIES (LDCs).

Eisenhower Doctrine—President Dwight Eisenhower's 1957 announcement that America would not permit further Communist advances in the Middle East. American troops landed in Lebanon in 1958 to enforce the Doctrine after outbreak of armed rebellion.

Escalation—Increased forces and intensity of war effort on one or both sides. One threat that haunts strategists is the potential escalation of a conventional war into a nuclear war.

European Communities (EC), or The Common Market, European Economic Community—The combination of Western Europe countries since 1958 to provide a large internal area for mutual trade regulated by complex, multilateral negotiations.

First Strike, or Preemptive Strike—Nuclear attack designed to surprise the enemy and destroy his capacity to retaliate in kind. A FIRST STRIKE would be directed against military targets: that is, COUNTER-FORCE, as opposed to COUNTER-VALUE, directed against civilian targets. FIRST STRIKE is not FIRST USE. FIRST USE is the use of nuclear arms before the enemy. The option of FIRST USE is intended to deter aggression on the part of the power with superior CONVENTIONAL FORCES.

Glasnost (Russian "openness")—Policy announced by Soviet leader Mikhail Gorbachev in 1986–87. It aimed at relaxing the strict controls on speech and information that had existed in the Soviet Union since Stalin's time. See PERESTROIKA.

Good Neighbor Policy—Policy of friendship and nonintervention announced by President Franklin D. Roosevelt in 1933, aimed at improving relations with Latin American countries. See ROOSEVELT COROLLARY TO THE MONROE DOCTRINE.

Group Theory—Ingroup-Outgroup Relations. Sociological concept used in analysis of international relations. Human beings are group-forming creatures. Each person is a member of various "ingroups" (family, school, labor union, religion, country). Members of ingroups tend to be suspicious or even hostile toward other groups, or out-groups. This concept is often applied to problems of international relations to explain suspicion, fear, hatred, and envy.

Heartland—According to Sir Halford Mackinder, a British geographer, the HEARTLAND is the area in Eurasia between the Elbe River and the Ural Mountains; it was the least vulnerable area in the world (at least before the development of ICBMs). Mackinder wrote:

> Who controls the Heartland commands the World Island
> Who controls the World Island commands the world.

By the WORLD ISLAND Mackinder means Eurasia and Africa, that is, the world's greatest compact land mass. See also RIMLAND.

Human Rights—Term popularized since World War II to describe rights of the individual citizen that all governments should respect. The United Nations promulgated the UNIVERSAL DECLARATION OF HUMAN RIGHTS in 1948, which included dozens of "rights and freedoms," political, intellectual, religious, and economic. Some of the rights conflict with others, and the document is ignored or flouted in much of the world. Another statement, the HELSINKI ACCORD (1971), was part of the process of détente. In return for Western recognition of Soviet gains in Europe, the Soviets were supposed to respect certain basic rights in areas under their control. Before the term HUMAN RIGHTS became popular, NATURAL RIGHTS or the RIGHTS OF MAN, connected with the idea of NATURAL LAW, predominated. See NATURAL LAW.

Ideology—(1) A way of thinking and set of ideas common to a group or culture. (2) Since the French Revolution, IDEOLOGY is used to describe a militant system of political ideas. Examples: NAZI ideology, COMMUNIST ideology.

Imperialism—Acquisition of territories and client states by a strong power, and/or a policy of expansion and conquest. LENIN argued that imperialism was the highest stage of CAPITALISM, as expanding industries attempted to secure foreign markets and raw materials. This is still a tenet of MARXISM-LENINISM, which denies that Communist expansion is "imperialistic."

Interventionism—Intervening in the affairs of other states, especially in internal conflicts that may threaten the peace and security of the intervening states. See BREZHNEV DOCTRINE, EISENHOWER DOCTRINE, ROOSEVELT COROLLARY TO THE MONROE DOCTRINE, and contrast ISOLATIONISM.

Isolationism—Policy of keeping international relations and responsibilities to the barest minimum. America followed this policy generally until 1941 ("no entangling alliances," Jefferson). America did not, however, isolate itself from the affairs of the American continents: witness the MONROE DOCTRINE, THE MEXICAN WAR, SPANISH-AMERICAN WAR, ROOSEVELT COROLLARY TO THE MONROE DOCTRINE.

Just War—A Christian concept that regulates the use of military force; defensive wars waged by legitimate sovereigns are just; not only must the *objective* be just, but the *means* must be proportional.

KGB *(Komitet Gosudarstvennoi Bezopasnosti*—Committee of State Security)—Abbreviation for the Soviet secret police and state intelligence agency since 1954. Its predecessors had various acronyms: Cheka, GPU, OGUP, NKVD, NKBB, MGB.

Logistics—The science of moving and supplying military forces.

Maoism—The version of MARXISM-LENINISM developed by MAO TSE-TUNG (Zedong), Communist leader of the People's Republic of China, 1949–1976. MAOISM stressed the role of peasants in a Marxist revolution, and the use of PROTRACTED GUERRILLA WARFARE. MAOISM came to stand for Communism independent of Moscow. MAO'S ideas were adopted in various forms in many countries, and produced splits in several Communist parties. Maoism is associated also with erratic changes of Communist policy marked by movements such as "The Great Leap Forward," "Let a Hundred Flowers Bloom," and "The Cultural Revolution." See MARXISM-LENINISM, STALINISM.

Marxism-Leninism—The philosophy behind Soviet Communist ideology; a combination of Karl Marx's nineteenth-century doctrine of proletarian revolution against bourgeois capitalism and Vladimir I. Lenin's application of the revolution in underdeveloped conditions such as in Tsarist Russia in 1917 and in Third World countries today. Lenin also converted Marx's concept of "the dictatorship of the proletariat" to the dictatorship of an intensely disciplined, hierarchical, elitist Communist party. See also STALINISM, MAOISM.

Missiles—Term now mainly used for ballistic (rocket-propelled) nuclear explosives and cruise missiles. The main classes of missiles are:
    Intercontinental Ballistic Missiles (ICBM)—Long range missiles (6,000–9,000 miles) capable of delivering warheads between Eurasia and the Americas.
    Intermediate Range Nuclear Forces (INF)—Missiles with ranges from

600 to 3,400 miles, suited to attacks within the confines of Eurasia and North Africa, such as the Soviet SS20 and SS4, or the U.S. Pershing II, and cruise missiles—ground-launched, sea-launched, and air-launched (GLCM, SLCM, ALCM).

Short-Range Missiles (SRBM)—Their range is between 45 and 600 miles.

Multiple Independently Targetable Reentry Vehicle (MIRV)—Missile with a number of warheads each of which can be independently directed—one rocket can deliver attacks on ten separate targets.

Monroe Doctrine—Announced December 1823 by President James Monroe. European powers may not encroach on the American Hemisphere or extend European political systems there. The United States will not interfere with existing European colonies nor intervene in European wars. See ROOSEVELT COROLLARY TO THE MONROE DOCTRINE and CUBAN MISSILE CRISIS.

Moral Equivalance or Moral Symmetry—The assumption that there is no moral difference between rival great powers, since all great powers are out for their NATIONAL INTEREST. Thus the motives and aims of the United States are no better and no worse than those of the Soviet Union, and the spread of democracy is merely a cover for American imperialism, just as the expansion of Communism is an instrument of Soviet imperialism. By the same argument there was no moral difference between Nazi Germany and Britain, or between Japan and America in World War II. See NATIONAL INTEREST, NATURAL LAW, REALPOLITIK, REVISIONISM.

Most Favored Nation Clause—In international trade agreements, parties to the agreement will give the same privileges, such as lower TARIFFS, to each other as either gives to any other nation.

Multilateral (Latin: ''many-sided'')—An arrangement or agreement among a number of parties; especially applied to agreements among states; contrast BILATERAL—between two sides—and UNILATERAL—one-sided: a decision or action by one party/state without the consent of any other.

Munich Analogy—Argument from the consequences of the 1938 Munich Agreement, when the governments of Britain and France agreed to appease Hitler by letting his army take over Sudetenland (in Czechoslovakia), thus hoping to prevent a major war. Six months later, Hitler easily took the whole of Czechoslovakia, and five months after that (September 1939) invaded Poland—the beginning of World War II.

The MUNICH ANALOGY asserts that to prevent major wars one must be prepared to oppose and, if necessary, fight potential aggressors at an early stage. Contrast the VIETNAM ANALOGY.

Mutual Assured Destruction (MAD)—Policy to prevent a major war by the certainty that if either superpower attacks the other with nuclear weapons of mass destruction, retaliation will follow, and both sides will be destroyed. See BALANCE OF TERROR, DETERRENCE.

National Interest—Broad term meaning the security and prosperity of the country, which a government must protect. The NATIONAL INTEREST is often set in contrast to a MORALIZING or CRUSADING view of foreign policy. See REALPOLITIK.

National Security Council (NSC)—A group of presidential advisors who meet to assist the president in foreign policy questions. Originated under President Harry S. Truman. Its influence and operations have varied under successive presidents. The staff member who coordinates the council's work is the NATIONAL SECURITY ADVISOR.

Natural Law, or Law of Nature—The set of moral values thought to be shared by all reasonable, or rational, human beings. Such values are or ought to be the foundation of INTERNATIONAL LAW; they include the duty to keep promises, to use force only in just causes, to respect property earned by honest means, etc. Many modern theorists reject the idea of natural law, arguing that all binding rules must be enacted by a SOVEREIGN power, and/or that values are conventional, that is, vary from one society and culture to another. MARXISM-LENINISM asserts that values are imposed by the ruling class and that, therefore, Communists have no obligations toward the natural law as understood in non-Marxist societies.

Nazism—Abbreviation of NAZIONAL SOZIALISTISCHE DEUTSCHE ARBEITER PARTEI (National Socialist German Workers' Party). The ideology and policies of dictator Adolf Hitler and his collaborators. Fanatical patriotism, expansionism, and militarism, coupled with racial theories, including Aryan superiority and anti-Semitism. One result was World War II; another, the attempt to exterminate all Jews in Europe.

Neutrality—The policy of complete nonintervention by a state in the disputes and wars of other states.

Newspeak—*The Oxford American Dictionary* gives the following definition: ''vague and misleading language as used especially by government spokesmen trying to conceal truth and influence public opinion," and attributes it to George Orwell's *1984*. Orwell, however, seemed to be satirizing the Stalinist technique of giving certain words a peculiar meaning, well understood by party members, but designed to confuse outsiders. Extreme examples in *1984* were slogans such as "Freedom is Slavery" or "War is Peace." In the 1930s words such as "fascism," "anti-fascism," "imperialism," "people's democracy," "social fascism," and "popular front" became part of the Communist glossary of code words. The vocabulary has since been expanded to include cryptic double meanings for "peace," "war," "liberation," "war of liberation," "neo-colonialism," "peaceful co-existence," and many more. Ambiguous code words are no longer the monopoly of Marxists, however. Terms such as "values," "freedom," "racism," "repression," "life-style," "affirmative action," "social responsibility," and "critical thinking" attest the widespread employment of semantic ambiguity or NEWSPEAK.

Nixon Doctrine—A doctrine that called for self-help on the part of U.S. allies, and a shift of primary responsibility for regional security to those allies and other nations, with only residual American responsibility. The NIXON DOCTRINE was applied first and foremost to Vietnam; it was born of the U.S. desire to quit the war, and led to a policy of "Vietnamization" under which the South Vietnamese were called on to develop the power to defend themselves.

North Atlantic Treaty Organization (NATO)—Mutual-defense organization established in April 1949 to protect Western Europe against Soviet aggression. Today, NATO has sixteen members, including Canada and the United States.

Nuclear Proliferation—The spread of nuclear armaments to more countries. The NON-PROLIFERATION TREATY (1968) tried to stem the tide of proliferation, but in addition to America, Britain, China, France, and the Soviet Union it is fairly certain that the following countries have nuclear weapons: India, Pakistan, South Africa, and Israel. There are probably others.

Organization of American States (OAS)—formed in 1948, its members are the twenty-eight countries of the Americas, exclusive of Cuba (expelled 1962), who meet to promote intra-American cooperation and collective security.

Organization of Petroleum Exporting Countries (OPEC)—Formed in 1960, an international cartel designed to regulate oil prices.

Pacifism—A conviction that any use of force is wrong and a consequent refusal to be a part of any military or coercive action. PACIFISTS usually propose UNILATERAL DISARMAMENT. Individual PACIFISTS may be permitted, as CONSCIENTIOUS OBJECTORS, to refuse to serve in armed forces.

Perestroika (Russian: "restructuring")—Gorbachev's policy of introducing competition and some aspects of a market economy into the COMMAND ECONOMY of the Soviet Union. See also GLASNOST.

Reagan Doctrine—U.S. support of anti-Communist revolution—such as the Contras' or the Afghan rebels' efforts—or a revised policy of CONTAINMENT.

Realpolitik (German: "Realistic policy")—Foreign and defense policy founded on calculations of power, NATIONAL INTEREST, and military capability.

Revisionism—In recent studies of international affairs, a movement among historians to attribute the COLD WAR to American imperialism, not to Soviet expansionism.

Rimland—Concept developed by American geographer Nicholas Spykman in response to Mackinder's HEARTLAND theory. The RIMLAND is the coastal area of the WORLD ISLAND—Western Europe, Western and Southern Africa, Arabian Peninsula, Iran, India, Southeast Asia, Southern China, Japan. Spykman argued that unless the power controlling the HEARTLAND also got control of the RIMLAND it could not conquer the world. Spykman's theory bears closely upon the course of East-West relations and North-South relations since World War II.

Roosevelt Corollary to the Monroe Doctrine (1904)—Policy to forestall intervention by European powers to protect their interests in Latin American countries; the United States would act as police toward delinquent Latin American states.

Sanction—Economic or military action against a country to punish or coerce it; generally sanctions are collectively imposed by a group of states.

Sovereignty—The right of a state to control its territory and those persons under its jurisdiction without answering to any other state or organization.

Sphere of Influence—Geographical area in which a state asserts, and is sometimes acknowledged to have, special interests.

Stalinism—Policies and methods of Josef Stalin, dictator of the Soviet Union after the death of Lenin in 1924. Stalin ruled despotically until his death in 1953. Stalinism involved brutal one-man dictatorship supported by bureaucracy, terrorism, purges, show trials, and slave-labor.

Status Quo (Latin: short for STATUS QUO ANTE: "position which [existed] before [the present position]."")—In international politics it has two meanings: 1. maintaining the existing state of affairs: STATUS QUO POWERS are states that do not want more power or territory. 2. STATUS QUO ANTE is a policy of returning to the state of things as it was *before* certain events took place. For example, when the USSR agreed to withdraw its missile bases in Cuba in 1962, it agreed to return to the STATUS QUO ANTE. See CUBAN MISSILE CRISIS.

Strategic Defense Initiative (SDI)—Proposed system to destroy inter-continental (strategic) missiles in flight. Called by opponents "Star Wars."

Strategy—In international politics and war, the long-run aims and plans of states, as contrasted with TACTICS.

Superpowers—Name applied to the United States and Soviet Union since World War II, since their size and nuclear arsenals put them far ahead of all other powers. In the past there were usually a number of GREAT POWERS, but this category is now relatively unimportant.

Tactics—In politics and in military action the limited and short-term operations to attain short-term objectives. Contrast STRATEGY.

Tariff—Tax on imported goods, usually imposed for policy reasons; for example to protect domestic industry against foreign competition or to retaliate against unfair competition.

Terrorism—Use of violence—often indiscriminate killing and cruelty—as well as threats to break people's will to resist.

Third World—Describes those states that are neither members of either the developed "capitalist world" (First World) or the developed "Communist world" (Second World). THIRD WORLD states are UNDER-DEVELOPED, or LESS DEVELOPED COUNTRIES (LDCs).

Totalitarianism—Political system that claims total control of the lives of its subjects—political, economic, social, ideological, educational, informational, etc. Not to be confused with non-totalitarian DICTATOR-SHIPS.

Triadic Defense—Three types of nuclear response developed by the United States to ensure that *retaliation* for nuclear attack will be possible. The three types are: ICBMS, based on land in the United States; submarine-launched missiles (SLBMS) and sea-launched cruise missiles (SLCM); and air-launched bombs and missiles delivered by planes of Strategic Air Command (SAC)

Truman Doctrine—Enunciated by President Harry Truman in 1947; it required CONTAINMENT of Soviet IMPERIALISM, and promised U.S. aid to Greece and Turkey, with resistance to aggression elsewhere in Europe. This marked the beginning of the COLD WAR.

Verification—In ARMS CONTROL agreements, the systems enabling either side to make sure (verify) that the other side is honoring the agreement.

Vietnam Analogy—The argument used since the U.S. defeat in Vietnam that democracies cannot fight strategic wars because the people's will to win will break down. Contrast MUNICH ANALOGY. The fear of "more Vietnams" is sometimes called the *Vietnam syndrome.*

War—Conflict between states usually involving force. International law demands that war should be *declared* by one or both states. In the present century, however, most international conflicts are *undeclared.* Some current classifications of war:

    Cold War—Hostility and conflict of interest without organized military attacks; term used to describe U.S.–Soviet rivalry from 1947 until "détente" in the 1970s.

    Conventional War—Armed conflict without nuclear weapons.

    Guerrilla Warfare—(Spanish word meaning "little war")—conflict by irregular forces inside a state aimed at subverting the government; see WAR OF LIBERATION.

    Limited War—Conflict in which the objectives and often the means are limited, as contrasted with *total war,* which aims at complete defeat and surrender of the enemy.

    War of Liberation—Currently means a Soviet-sponsored rebellion to impose a Communist dictatorship in a country; also called *subversive war.*

    War Guilt—A term used after World War I attributing the responsi-

bility for the war to Germany and justifying penalties and REPARA-
TION payments against the vanquished. In his *History of World War
II*, B. H. Liddell Hart suggests that countries that fail to rearm and
so deter potential aggressors are as responsible for the resulting
conflict as the aggressor whom they tempted by their weakness.

International Events Chronology from 1945

This timeline is intended as a rough checklist for the chronological order of major events. It does not include all significant developments in world politics; nor does it indicate causal connections. For more recent events, consult current Information Please Almanac *or* World Almanac.

1945

February—Crimea *(Yalta)* Conference

February—*Death of President Roosevelt.* Vice President *Truman* becomes president.

April–June—*San Francisco Conference* sets up the United Nations

May—*Germany Capitulates*

July—*Potsdam Conference*

August—Atomic Bombs are dropped on Hiroshima and Nagasaki: *Japan Surrenders*

October—*United Nations* comes into formal existence

November—Soviet forces support Communist revolution in northern *Iran*

1946

March—Former Prime Minister Churchill speaks in Fulton, Missouri, using the term *Iron Curtain*

April—Soviet troops withdraw from Iran

May—Communist guerrillas wage civil war in Greece

July—The United States begins atomic tests at Bikini in the Marshall Islands

1947

January—America abandons mediation between nationalist and Communist Chinese

March—*Truman Doctrine* of economic aid and military aid to nations threatened by Communism: U.S. advisers sent to Greece; *Cold War Begins*

June—*Marshall Plan* proposed for economic recovery for war-torn nations of Europe

August—Independence for India and Pakistan

1948

April—Foreign Assistance Act initiates the Marshall Plan (European Recovery Program)

April—*Organization of American States* (OAS) meets

May—*Israel* becomes an independent state

June—Yugoslavia and USSR break relations

July—USSR imposes *Berlin Blockade* to protest currency reforms in West Germany. *Berlin Airlift* begins

August—Soviet Union breaks consular relations with the United States in protest against U.S. refusal to return a defector

December—*Universal Declaration of Human Rights* proclaimed by the United Nations

1949

January—*Harry S. Truman* inaugurated for second term

February—*USSR and Communist China* sign a thirty-year treaty of alliance

April—*North Atlantic Treaty Organization* (NATO) formed to guaranteed assistance against aggression. Members include the United States, Great Britain, France, Belgium, Netherlands, Luxemburg, Italy, Portugal, Denmark, Iceland, Norway, and Canada. (Greece and Turkey joined in 1952, West Germany in 1955, and Spain in 1982.)

May—*Berlin Blockade* lifted

June—U.S. forces withdraw from Korea

July—Vatican excommunicates all Catholics who support Communist doctrine

September—*Berlin Airlift* ends

September—USSR repudiates 1945 treaty of friendship with Yugoslavia

October—*People's Republic of China* (PRC) comes into existence under *Mao Tse-tung* (Zedong); America refuses to recognize it

October—Bulgaria, Poland, and Romania denounce their treaty of friendship with Yugoslavia

December—Vietnam becomes an associated state of the French Union

December—Chinese Nationalist forces retreat to Taiwan (Formosa); Communists control all mainland China

December—Independence of Indonesia

1950

January—Truman authorizes development of hydrogen bomb

June—Invasion of South Korea by North Korea. United Nations (including the United States) enters the *Korean War*

July—U.S. ground forces return to Korea

September—U.N. and U.S. troops land at Inchon, South Korea, and press towards Seoul

October—U.N. troops cross the 38th parallel into North Korea.

November—Chinese Communists invade Korea and stage a massive counteroffensive: U.N. troops retreat

1951

April—America provides military aid to the Chinese Nationalist Government for the legitimate self-defense of Taiwan

May—U.S.-Iceland agreement provides use of defense facilities for NATO

September—Peace treaty with Japan

December—Economic recovery of Western Europe: end of Marshall Plan

1952

February—*Greece* and *Turkey* join NATO

February—King George VI of Britain dies; Elizabeth II crowned

July—Puerto Rico becomes a commonwealth under U.S. jurisdiction

August—USSR tests a 40-megaton atomic high-altitude bomb

October—Successful test of atomic bomb by Britain

November—America detonates first *hydrogen bomb*

1953

January—*Dwight D. Eisenhower* inaugurated

March 2—*Stalin Dies,* Georgi M. Malenkov becomes first secretary

March—*Nikita Khrushchev* succeeds Malenkov as party leader (and real head of Soviet government)

July—At Panmunjon, Korea, an armistice is signed by the U.N. and North Korean officials, ending a two-year stalemate at the 38th parallel

August—USSR explodes its first H-bomb

1954

June—Vietminh defeat French at *Dienbienphu.* Ho Chi Minh's Communist government controls North Vietnam

June—Ngo Dinh Diem becomes premier of South Vietnam: U.S. military advisers in South Vietnam

March—America signs mutual defense treaty with Japan

September—First nuclear-powered submarine

October—End of allied military occupation of West Germany

December—United States and Taiwan sign a mutual-defense treaty

1955

January—Republic of Panama and America sign a treaty in which both agree to cooperate on issues pertaining to the Panama Canal

April—Bandung Conference of unaligned nations (called by Sukarno, president of Indonesia)

May—West Germany formally admitted to NATO

May—*Warsaw Pact* established to counter NATO. Members: Bulgaria, Czechoslovakia, East Germany, Hungary, Poland, Albania, Romania, and the USSR (Albania dropped out in 1968)

May—USSR annuls treaties of friendship with Britain and France

July—Austria regains its sovereignty; end of military occupation

September—Southeast Asia Treaty Organization (SEATO) formed (Australia, Britain, France, New Zealand, Pakistan, Philippines, Thailand, America). Ineffective as regional security pact

December—Admission of Ireland, Bulgaria, and Hungary to the United Nations

1956

May—United States explodes the first airborn hydrogen bomb

July—Withdrawal of Soviet occupation forces from Romania

July—Egypt nationalizes the Suez Canal in retaliation for U.S. withdrawal of funds from the Aswan Dam project

November—Soviet troops crush anti-Soviet revolt in Hungary

November—*Suez War:* Britain, France, and Israel attack Egypt. America compels a cease-fire in the Sinai Peninsula and withdrawal of the invasion.

1957

January—*Eisenhower* inaugurated for second term

January—*Eisenhower Doctrine:* no further spread of Communism in the Middle East

March—Ghana gains independence: the first "New African Nation"

March—*Rome Treaty* establishes the European Economic Community (or Common Market), effective in 1958

May—Britain detonates its first hydrogen bomb

October—Soviet Union launches the first man-made earth satellite (Sputnik I)

December—Establishment of NATO missile bases in Europe under U.S. control

1958

February—Cyprus gains independence

July—Eight thousand troops land in Lebanon in response to crisis in Middle East (Eisenhower Doctrine)

July—United States and Canada create a joint-defense committee

October—United States withdraws troops from Lebanon

1959

January—Castro overthrows Cuban dictator Batista; America recognizes Castro's government on Cuba

March—People's Republic of China invades and annexes Tibet

May—Beginning of estrangement between USSR and PRC

June—Greece rejects a Soviet note urging no missile bases be established in Greece.

December—*Antarctic Treaty:* Antarctica to be reserved for scientific and peaceful activities

1960

South Vietnam infiltrated by Viet Cong guerrillas, including North Vietnamese forces

Organization of Petroleum Exporting Countries (OPEC): this oil cartel aims at coordinating oil production in order to control prices

February—French explode atomic bomb

May—Open break between the Soviet Union and Communist China

May—U.S. reconnaissance plane (U-2) shot down in Soviet Russia. Khrushchev uses incident to break up the Paris peace talks

July—U.S. cuts imports of sugar from Cuba by 95 per cent; Castro now clearly a Communist dictator

October—Nigeria gains independence

1961

January—*Kennedy* inauguarated

January—America breaks ties with Castro's Cuba

April—*Bay of Pigs* invasion of Cuba fails

April—Major Yuri A. Gagarin, of the Soviet Union, is the first man to orbit the earth (Vostok I)

May—*Alliance for Progress* established to help Latin America

June—Kennedy-Khrushchev "summit" in Vienna

July—East-West confrontation in Berlin

August—East Germany builds the *Berlin Wall* to prevent exodus to West Germany

August—USSR announces the resumption of nuclear testing

1962

February—John Glenn first American to orbit the earth (Mercury Space Capsule)

February—Total ban on U.S. trade with Cuba

October—USSR explodes a 50-plus megaton hydrogen bomb

October—*Cuban Missile Crisis*

1963

May—Kennedy and Canadian Prime Minister Pearson agree to equip Canadian missiles with U.S.-supplied nuclear warheads

August—*"Hot Line"* set up between U.S. and the USSR

November—USSR launches first maneuverable unmanned satellite

November 1—Diem (premier of South Vietnam) overthrown with U.S. knowledge and assassinated

November 22—*Assassination of President Kennedy.* Vice President Lyndon B. Johnson takes oath of office as president

December—Kenya gains independence

1964

January—Anti-American riots in the Panama Canal Zone

August—*Gulf of Tonkin Incident and Resolution*

October—Deposition of Khrushchev. Leonid Brezhnev becomes leader of the Soviet Union

1965

January—PRC begins violent purge known as the *Great Cultural Revolution*

March—Lieutenant Colonel Aleksei A. Leonov, in the Soviet spacecraft Voskhod II, is the first human being to walk in space

March—Johnson commits America to major combat role in Vietnam

April—marines sent to *Dominican Republic* to check military coup and possible Communist takeover

June—America begins mass bombing in Vietnam

October—U.S. internal opposition to the Vietnam War begins. Ho Chi Minh comments that the war will not be won on the battlefield but on the streets of San Francisco and New York

1966

June—first bombing of *Hanoi* and *Haiphong*

September—aerial defoliation of areas in the north of South Vietnam to prevent infiltration of fighters and arms from North Vietnam

1967

January—*Treaty of Principles Governing the Activities of the States* in the exploration of outer space—prohibits the orbiting of weapons of mass destruction and forbids all claims of territories

March—France withdraws troops from NATO command and requests all NATO bases be removed from France. France still remains a member of NATO

April—Coup by a group of rightist army officials in Greece. U.S. embargo on military supplies to Greece

June—Israel-Arab *Six-Day* war; rapid and complete Israeli victory

June—General Agreement on Tariffs and Trade (GATT)

December—U.S. now has 474,000 troops in Vietnam and Thailand

1968

January—*U.S.S. Pueblo* seized by North Korea

January—*Tet Offensive* in Vietnam. Major losses by North Vietnam. U.S. media portray the battle as a defeat for U.S. forces, thus increasing opposition to the war

February—U.S. forces retake *Hue*

May—Peace talks begin in Paris between the America and North Vietnam

June—*Nuclear Non-Proliferation Treaty*

July—Direct air service between America and the USSR

August—*Invasion of Czechoslovakia* by the USSR and other Warsaw Pact nations. Romania refuses to send troops to help suppress Czechoslovakia's attempt at a more humane Communist system

September—Albania withdraws from the *Warsaw Pact*

1969

January—*Richard Nixon* inaugurated

July—First landing on the moon

August—Lt. Col. Qaddafi seizes power as dictator of Libya

November—Agreement between the United States and Japan for the return of Okinawa to Japan in 1972

November—News reports of *My Lai* massacre (a U.S. officer ordered executions of civilian villagers in Vietnam)

November—*Strategic Arms Limitations Talks* (SALT) begin

1970

During the 1970s international terrorism becomes a serious menace that the great powers seem unable to prevent

April—President Nixon announces the commitment of U.S. troops to attack enemy bases in Cambodia

May—Four students at Kent State University are killed by National Guardsmen during a protest

September—Termination of U.S. military embargo on Greece

December—Riots in Gdansk and other port cities of Poland

1971

January–U.S. détente with USSR begins; West Germany engages in *Ostpolitik*

June—America lifts 21-year embargo on trade with the People's Republic of China

November—People's Republic of China replaces Nationalist China (Taiwan) in the United Nations

December—America resumes heavy bombing in North Vietnam

1972

January—American troops in Vietnam are reduced to 69,000. Vietnamization near completion

February—Nixon visits People's Republic of China

March—North Vietnam conducts massive invasion of SouthVietnam. America renews bombing of North Vietnam, which has been suspended for three years

May—America mines North Vietnam's ports

May—Nixon visits USSR: the first peacetime visit to the Soviet Union by an American president. SALT I signed

June—Terrorist massacre of Israelis at Munich Olympic Games

July—Nixon sets trade deal to sell grain to USSR

August—Salt I confirmed by the Senate: includes Anti-Ballistic Missile (ABM) Treaty

August—Last American troops leave South Vietnam

December—Bombing of NorthVietnam is resumed to encourage cease-fire

1973

January—Peace agreement and ceasefire with North Vietnam

June—Investigation of *Watergate* break-in begins

October—Egypt invades Israel: *Yom Kippur War*

October—Vice President Spiro Agnew resigns and is replaced by *Gerald R. Ford*

October—Oil embargo imposed by Arab nations: severe oil shortage in United States

November—United States resumes diplomatic relations with Egypt

November—Congress passes the *War Powers Act* over Nixon's veto: serious limitation of powers of the commander-in-chief

1974

March—End of oil embargo

June—Nixon visits USSR for summit talk, no results

August—President Nixon resigns. President Gerald Ford sworn in

September—President Ford pardons former President Nixon

1975

April—South Vietnam, denied aid by vote of Congress, is overrun by North Vietnam army; fall of Saigon, renamed Ho Chi Minh City.

April—Communist government in Cambodia (*Khmer Rouge*) begins massacres that wipe out one-tenth of the population

May—American cargo ship *Mayaguez* is captured by Cambodian government (Communist) troops. President Ford orders successful rescue operation

July—*Helsinki Accords:* USSR agrees to respect human rights (but fails to do so)

November—Angola and Mozambique become independent; Cuban troops establish Communist government in Angola

December—President Ford visits East Asia—PRC, Indonesia, Philippines

1976

May—Limited nuclear test ban agreed on by superpowers

September—Death of Mao Zedong: succeeded by Hua Guofeng after a brief power struggle

1977

January—*Jimmy Carter* inaugurated—issues pardon to Vietnam War draft evaders

February—President Carter makes human rights major issue in U.S. foreign policy decision making

March—Carter says U.S. ground forces in Korea will be withdrawn within five years (Carter administration subsequently recanted)

June—*Neutron* bomb is proposed by United States for use in defense of Europe, but later abandoned

September—Treaty for gradual return of *Panama Canal Zone* to Panama

1978

April—President Carter cancels production of *Neutron* bomb

September—*Camp David Accords* between Israel and Egypt mediated by President Carter

November—America permits 47,000 refugees from Southeast Asia to enter the country, the "boat people"

1979

January—Overthrow of the *Shah of Iran;* rise of *Khomeini*

January—U.S. opens diplomatic relations with PRC and breaks official relations with Nationalist China (Taiwan)

March—Israel and Egypt sign peace treaty—had been in "state of war" since 1948

May—Dictator Somoza is overthrown in Nicaragua, after America withdraws aid. *Sandinistas in power* with Cuban and Soviet support

July—SALT II treaty signed by President Carter and Soviet President Leonid Brezhnev. Not ratified by U.S. Senate owing to the Soviet invasion of Afghanistan in December of 1979

November—"Students" in Iran, now under the fanatical Shi-ite dictatorship of Khomeini, capture U.S. *Embassy in Teheran* and held 90 diplomatic personnel hostages

December—*Soviet invasion of Afghanistan* to support puppet Communist government against the rebels. End of "détente"

1980

January—Carter cancels grain shipment to the USSR and calls for other sanctions against USSR for invading Afghanistan

April—Mugabe elected prime minister of Zimbabwe

April—American hostage rescue mission to Iran fails

September—*Iraq* invades *Iran*

1981

January—*President Ronald Reagan* inaugurated

January—After 444 days of captivity, U.S. hostages in Iran are released

March—America sends aid to President Jose Napoleon Duarte in El Salvador

May—*Daniel Ortega's* Sandinistas control Nicaragua

July—Israel and the PLO sign cease-fire agreement

August—South African troops enter Angola on a campaign against guerrillas

August—U.S. planes shoot down two Libyan fighters off Libyan coast

October—Anwar el-Sadat of Egypt is assassinated

December—President Reagan asks all U.S. citizens to leave Libya and blocks all U.S. passports to that country

December—Reagan announces U.S. will train 1,000 Salvadoran soldiers to fight leftist insurgents

1982

February—1,000 additional U.N. soldiers will be sent to Southern Lebanon to preserve a ceasefire along Lebanon-Israeli borders

March—America releases a report that the USSR is using chemical warfare in Afghanistan

April—Argentina sends armed forces to seize the *Falkland Islands*, a British possession. Britain surrounds the Falklands and begins an air and sea blockade

June—Israelis attack Southern Lebanon by sea, air, and land

June—Argentine forces surrender to the British in the Falklands

July—Iranian troops move into Iraq in a major offensive

August—U.S. marines land in Beirut to take part in peace-keeping efforts in Lebanon

1983

April—Space Shuttle's maiden voyage

August—Philippines opposition leader Benigno Aquino, Jr., is killed at Manila's airport

September—The Soviet Union shoots down a commercial airplane of Korean Airlines over Kamchatka, killing 269

October—France sends jet fighters to Iraq to help in the Iranian-Iraq War

October—Terrorists blow up U.S. marine headquarters in Beirut

October—United States liberates *Grenada* following a coup by pro-Soviet local Communists

November—America decides to withdraw from UNESCO

December—Democratic government begins in Argentina

December—Military seizes power in Nigeria

1984

February—Reagan pulls marines out of Beirut after terrorist bombing in which more than 200 Americans died

April—Reagan visits Mainland China

September—U.S. embassy in Beirut bombed by terrorists

1985

March—*Mikhail S. Gorbachev* becomes leader of the USSR

September—Under pressure from Congress, President Reagan announces *Sanctions Against South Africa,* for apartheid

November—*Geneva Summit:* Reagan and Gorbachev

December—Britain joins America in leaving UNESCO

1986

February—In the Philippines, Marcos rule ends after twenty years; Corazon Aquino takes control of the government

February—Jean-Claude Duvalier (Baby Doc) flees Haiti after months of economic unrest; six-member army governing council takes control

March—U.S. armed clash with Libya in the Gulf of Sidra

April—U.S. planes bomb Libya in retaliation for bombing of a German night club in which 155 were wounded and two killed

April—Nuclear power plant at *Chernobyl* in USSR melts down, releasing radiation in USSR and Europe

June—Congress votes $100 million in military aid and economic aid to the *Contras* (Freedom Fighters) opposing the Sandinista government in Nicaragua

October—Rejkjavik "Summit"' Gorbachev and Reagan fail to agree on arms reduction

November—U.S. secret arms deal with Iran and covert supplies to Nicaraguan contras becomes public

1987

April—Gorbachev announces that USSR will agree to removal of INF from European theater. Renewed, complex negotiations

May—Congressional investigation of *Iran-Contra* aid begins

May—*U.S.S. Stark* is hit by Iranian Exocet missiles fired by Iraqi plane in Persian Gulf: America plans defensive patrols to protect oil tankers and forestall Soviet intrusion in the gulf

June—Riots in South Korea

June—The *de facto* leader of Panama, General Manuel Noriega is accused of crimes including drug-smuggling. Strained relations between the United States and Panama

August—Various "peace" plans for Nicaragua's Civil War

August—Libyan forces are driven out of Chad, after fourteen years of occupation of northern territory

September—Negotiations for ban on INF missiles continue

November—Gorbachev denounces the enormous crimes of Stalin

November—Ortega proposed cease-fire with contras in Nicaragua. Talks soon break down

December—Reagan and Gorbachev sign, in Washington, the INF Treaty, eliminating all superpowers' medium-range nuclear forces (Soviet SS-20s, U.S. Pershing IIs, and Ground Launched Cruise Missiles.)

December—Violent Palestinian protests in Israeli occupied territory. These protests continue through 1988

1988

January—Soviets announce they will gradually withdraw Soviet forces from Afghanistan. (Invasion began in December 1979, and led to more than eight years of guerrilla resistance.)

February—House of Representatives refused to vote aid ($36.25 million) to the contras in Nicaragua, 219–211

February—Dictator of Panama, Noriega, indicted in U.S. courts for drug trafficking. Turmoil and economic chaos in Panama; U.S. refused to intervene militarily

March—Sandinista government in Nicaragua and contras agree to a truce, but leftist guerrillas continue to operate in El Salvador

March—Unrest in Soviet Armenia

March—Mengistu, Marxist dictator of Ethiopia, resumes genocide by famine

April—No progress to peace in Nicaragua

May—Labor unrest in Poland

May—Reagan and Gorbachev have their fourth summit in Moscow. No major achievement

June—Economic summit of Western developed states in Toronto, Canada

July—U.S. warship shoots down an Iranian passenger plane over the Persian Gulf

July—U.N. proposal to end Iraq-Iran War accepted by Iran

July—Jordan, nominal sovereign of Israeli-occupied West Bank, transfers sovereignty to the Palestine Liberation Organization (PLO)

August—Cessation of hostilities in Angola and Namibia. Proposed withdrawl of Cuban troops from Angola and South Africans from Namibia

August—Cease-fire in Iran-Iraq War

October—Changes in Soviet government. Gorbachev called president

November—George Bush elected president of the United States

November—Symbolic of glasnost: Soviet dissident Andrei Sakharov visits the United States.

December—Gorbachev addresses U.N. General Assembly in New York: proposes troop and arms reduction in Europe

December—Devastating earthquake in Soviet Armenia: many nations contribute supplies and rescue teams

Index of Names

WIDENER UNIVERSITY
WOLFGRAM
LIBRARY
CHESTER, PA.